Michael Smit

Privacy in e-Commerce Software

Michael Smit

Privacy in e-Commerce Software

Benefiting from protecting consumer privacy

VDM Verlag Dr. Müller

Bibliografische Information der Deutschen Nationalbibliothek:
Die Deutsche Nationalbibliothek verzeichnet diese Publikation in der Deutschen
Nationalbibliografie; detaillierte bibliografische Daten sind im Internet über
http://dnb.d-nb.de abrufbar.

Das Werk ist einschließlich aller seiner Teile urheberrechtlich geschützt. Jede
Verwertung außerhalb der engen Grenzen des Urheberrechtsgesetzes ist ohne
Zustimmung des Verlages unzulässig und strafbar. Das gilt insbesondere für
Vervielfältigungen, Übersetzungen, Mikroverfilmungen und die Einspeicherung
und Verarbeitung in elektronischen Systemen.

Alle in diesem Buch genannten Marken und Produktnamen unterliegen waren-
zeichen-, marken- oder patentrechtlichem Schutz bzw. sind Warenzeichen oder
eingetragene Warenzeichen der jeweiligen Inhaber. Die Wiedergabe von Marken,
Produktnamen, Gebrauchsnamen, Handelsnamen, Warenbezeichnungen u.s.w. in
diesem Werk berechtigt auch ohne besondere Kennzeichnung nicht zu der
Annahme, dass solche Namen im Sinne der Warenzeichen- und Markenschutz-
gesetzgebung als frei zu betrachten wären und daher von jedermann benutzt
werden dürften.

Copyright © 2007 VDM Verlag Dr. Müller e. K. und Lizenzgeber
Alle Rechte vorbehalten. Saarbrücken 2007
Kontakt: VDM Verlag Dr. Müller e.K., Dudweiler Landstr. 125 a,
D-66123 Saarbrücken, Telefon +49 681/9100-698, Telefax +49 681/9100-988
Email: info@vdm-verlag.de
Coverbild: copyright www.purestockx.com
Covererstellung: Christian Müller

Herstellung:
Schaltungsdienst Lange o.H.G., Zehrensdorfer Str. 11, D-12277 Berlin
Books on Demand GmbH, Gutenbergring 53, D-22848 Norderstedt

ISBN: 978-3-8364-2252-9

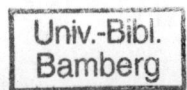

To my family, who got me here, and to my supervisors and colleagues, who helped me leave.

Table of Contents

List of Tables vi

List of Figures vii

Abstract x

List of Abbreviations Used xi

Glossary xiii

Acknowledgements xvii

Chapter 1		Introduction	1
Chapter 2		Background and Related Work	5
2.1	Privacy and the Knowledge Economy		5
	2.1.1	Definitions of privacy	6
		2.1.1.1 Personal information	8
		2.1.1.2 Confidentiality	8
	2.1.2	Privacy in legislation	9
	2.1.3	Privacy and public opinion	12
2.2	Commerce, Privacy, and Policy		15
	2.2.1	The e-economy	15
	2.2.2	Electronic commerce	16
	2.2.3	e-Commerce stakeholders' privacy views and requirements	18
	2.2.4	Privacy non-compliance consequences for e-commerce enterprises	21
	2.2.5	IBM® WebSphere® Commerce	22
	2.2.6	Business policy management	24
		2.2.6.1 Policy and privacy	25
	2.2.7	Privacy impact assessments	25
2.3	Technology and Privacy		27

	2.3.1	Privacy enhancing technologies in e-commerce		27
		2.3.1.1	Platform for privacy preferences (P3P)	27
		2.3.1.2	Privacy software tools for consumers	30
		2.3.1.3	Privacy seal programs	31
		2.3.1.4	Enterprise privacy authorization language	32
		2.3.1.5	Privacy software tools and services for enterprises	33
	2.3.2	Software testing		34
		2.3.2.1	Risk-based decisions	35
	2.3.3	Security threat models		36
	2.3.4	Privacy risk modeling for ubiquitous computer systems		38
2.4	Summary			38

Chapter 3   Methodology   40

3.1	Hypotheses			40
3.2	Enterprise Privacy Policies			41
	3.2.1	Enterprise privacy policy management		42
		3.2.1.1	Requirements of a privacy policy management framework	43
		3.2.1.2	Framework for enterprise privacy policy management	44
	3.2.2	Set of policy resources		46
		3.2.2.1	Properties of the set of policy resources	47
		3.2.2.2	Properties of a policy resource	47
		3.2.2.3	Properties of a policy rule	49
		3.2.2.4	Policy resources	50
	3.2.3	The enterprise and policy creation		56
		3.2.3.1	Assumptions for privacy policy creation	57
		3.2.3.2	Systematic approach to policy creation	58
	3.2.4	Resultant privacy policies		60
	3.2.5	Validation, verification, deployment, and enforcement		62
		3.2.5.1	Testing software applications for privacy policy compliance	63
		3.2.5.2	Privacy compliance testing methodology	71

3.3	Summary		72

Chapter 4   **Implementation and Results** **75**
- 4.1 Enterprise Privacy Policy Creation 75
  - 4.1.1 Privacy legislation 76
  - 4.1.2 Existing enterprise privacy policy 77
- 4.2 Testing Software Applications for Privacy Compliance 78
  - 4.2.1 Information flow markup language (IFML) 80
  - 4.2.2 Capture component: capture information flows 83
  - 4.2.3 Abstraction component: understand information flows 89
  - 4.2.4 Analysis component: rule evaluation 94
  - 4.2.5 Display component: report on compliance 97
    - 4.2.5.1 XML transformations 97
    - 4.2.5.2 SAX-like parsing 100
- 4.3 Privacy Compliance Testing Results 101
  - 4.3.1 Test environment 101
  - 4.3.2 Testing information flows 102
  - 4.3.3 Performance of privacy compliance testing 104
  - 4.3.4 Extensibility of the implementation 106
- 4.4 Summary 107

Chapter 5   **Conclusion** **108**
- 5.1 Hypotheses 111
- 5.2 Future Work 112

Bibliography **114**

Appendix A   **XML Schema Documents (XSD)** **125**
- A.1 IFML XSD 125
- A.2 XSD Describing Mapping Files 126

Appendix B   **XML Stylesheet Documents (XSLs)** **127**
- B.1 Overview Stylesheet 127
- B.2 Detailed Overview Stylesheet 128
- B.3 Individual Component View Stylesheet 128

List of Tables

Table 2.1	Comparison of OECD, European Union DPD, and Canada's PIPEDA privacy guidelines	12
Table 4.1	Requirements manually derived from legislation, with the severity of violations (warning or error).	77
Table 4.2	Most common action verbs in *PIPEDA*.	78
Table 4.3	Criteria for deriving requirements from P3P policies.	78
Table 4.4	Exemplar rules translated from the legislative rules (Table 4.1) and the P3P rules (Table 4.3).	96
Table 4.5	The rules enforced by this implementation and the tests used to verify violations can be detected.	103
Table 4.6	The response time of the web application for three tasks, with and without a filter.	105
Table 4.7	The running times of the abstraction component for IFML documents of varying size.	105
Table 4.8	The running times of the display component for IFML documents of varying size.	106

List of Figures

Figure 2.1   General privacy concern since 1978 (data from [78]).   13

Figure 2.2   General and Internet privacy concern in India, compared with 1998 survey of American Internet users.   14

Figure 2.3   Value of Internet Sales in Canada from 2001-2005 (data from [109]).   17

Figure 2.4   A set of interactions in an e-commerce transaction: ordering, payment, delivery, all governed by a set of regulations.   18

Figure 2.5   WebSphere Commerce workflow diagram for the shopping workflow and the order product sub-workflow [65].   19

Figure 2.6   The high-level view of the main stakeholders in an e-commerce B2C model.   19

Figure 3.1   An overall view of enterprise privacy policy management. . . .   42

Figure 3.2   The enterprise privacy policy management framework.   45

Figure 3.3   Policy resources that influence enterprise privacy policies. . . .   46

Figure 3.4   The set of policy resources (a), containing policy resources (b) which contain privacy policies (c) comprised of privacy policy rules (d).   48

Figure 3.5   Exemplar policy resources and how they can influence enterprise privacy policies.   51

Figure 3.6   The overlap of four sample contributing sets.   52

Figure 3.7   Components of the exemplar 'laws' policy resource.   52

Figure 3.8   Components of the exemplar 'enterprise' policy resource. . . .   54

Figure 3.9   Components of the exemplar 'consumer requirements' policy resource.   54

Figure 3.10   Components of the exemplar 'industry standards' policy resource.   55

Figure 3.11 Components of the exemplar 'contracts' policy resource. 56

Figure 3.12 The enterprise, the enterprise subsets (called *retailers*), and the policy resources that influence each retailer. 57

Figure 3.13 An example of determining the weights of individual privacy policy rules based on three sample policy resources, $s_1, s_2,$ and s_3. 59

Figure 3.14 Determining the weights of individual privacy policies using the matrix method. 60

Figure 3.15 A concrete example of using the matrix method to determine the weights of individual privacy policies. 61

Figure 3.16 The privacy policies that result from policy creation. 62

Figure 3.17 The policy must be validated with the original policy resources and deployed. 64

Figure 3.18 Workflow for creating an order on an e-commerce website (modified from [67]), showing the privacy monitor filters. 66

Figure 3.19 Workflow for processing an e-commerce order (modified from [68]) showing the privacy monitor filters. 67

Figure 3.20 Example information handlers in e-commerce. 68

Figure 3.21 Communication medium for flows of information in an example e-commerce transaction. 70

Figure 3.22 Overall view of enterprise privacy policy management. 73

Figure 4.1 The two modules of the enterprise privacy policy management software framework implemented in this chapter. 76

Figure 4.2 The components that comprise the proof-of-concept implementation of privacy compliance testing. 80

Figure 4.3 The interface hierarchy with the base implementation class that full implementations can extend. 81

Figure 4.4 The factory objects that locate and return components. 81

Figure 4.5	The XML outline of an IFML document.	82
Figure 4.6	UML class diagram for the IFML Helper class.	84
Figure 4.7	A basic customer interaction with a J2EE application.	85
Figure 4.8	A customer's interaction with a J2EE application as modified to capture requests and responses.	87
Figure 4.9	UML class dependency diagram for the capture component implementation, CaptureFilter.	89
Figure 4.10	UML Class dependency diagram for the abstraction component implementations.	91
Figure 4.11	A simple XML file mapping a set of data descriptors to a single abstracted data label.	92
Figure 4.12	The variables, operators, and values that make up compliance tuples for the rule-based analysis.	95
Figure 4.13	The UML class dependency diagram for the analysis component.	97
Figure 4.14	The UML class dependency diagram for the display components.	98
Figure 4.15	Sample output from the individual.xsl XML transformation to HTML, after rendering.	99
Figure 4.16	Sample output from the overview.xsl XML transformation to HTML, after rendering.	100
Figure 4.17	Sample output from the detailed-overview.xsl XML transformation to HTML, after rendering.	100

Abstract

This research describes a framework and methodology for managing the privacy policy of an enterprise, including creation (based on factors like privacy legislation and consumer preferences), validation and verification, deployment and enforcement, and compliance testing for business processes and software. To validate the framework, two modules (creation and compliance testing) are implemented for an existing prominent electronic commerce software application.

A sample privacy policy is created based on privacy legislation and a business' privacy promises. Our unique approach monitors the personal information sent and received by the software application, converts it to a standardized representation. At defined points in the electronic commerce workflow, the transmissions are compared to a set of privacy rules to ascertain compliance. Non-compliant transmissions of personal information are privacy infractions and are addressed by stopping the workflow or by generating a report and alerting the administrator.

List of Abbreviations Used

ADL	Abstracted Data Label
API	Application Programming Interface
ATG	Art Technology Group
B2B	Business-to-Business electronic commerce
B2C	Business-to-Consumer electronic commerce
CIO	Chief Information Officer
DD	Data Descriptor
DOM	Document Object Model
DREAD	Damage Potential, Reproducibility, Exploitability, Affected users, Discoverability
E2E	Enterprise-to-Enterprise electronic commerce
EJB	Enterprise Java Bean
EPIC	Electronic Privacy Information Center
FERPA	Family Education Rights and Privacy Act
FTC	Federal Trade Commission (United States)
HIPAA	Health Insurance Portability and Accountability Act
HTML	Hypertext Markup Language
HTTP	Hypertext Transport Protocol
HTTPS	Hypertext Transport Protocol, Secure
ICT	Information and Communications Technology
IFML	Information Flow Markup Language

ISO	International Standards Organization
J2EE	Java Enterprise Edition
JRC	Joint Research Centre (European Union)
OECD	Organisation for Economic Cooperation and Development
P3P	Platform for Privacy Preferences
PCTIFML	Privacy Compliance Testing Information Flow Markup Language
PIA	Privacy Impact Assessment
PIPEDA	Personal Information Protection and Electronic Documents Act
SAX	Simple API for XML
SQL	Sequential Query Language
SSH	Secure Shell
SSL	Secure Sockets Layer
TBCS	Treasury Board of Canada Secretariat
UMG	Universal Media Group
UML	Unified Modeling Language
URL	Uniform Resource Locator
W3C	World Wide Web Consortium
XML	Extensible Markup Language
XSL	Extensible Stylesheet Language
XSLT	Extensible Stylesheet Language Transformations

Glossary

PIPEDA — The *Personal Information Protection and Electronic Documents Act*, Canada's federal privacy legislation.

***de facto* standard** — A standard that exists because it is widely used or widely accepted by a group of companies, though not enforced by any entity.

B2B — Business-to-business electronic commerce

B2C — Business-to-consumer electronic commerce

business — A particular company or corporation.

camelCase — A standard naming convention for variables in Java applications when the variable is a phrase or compound word.

check out or checkout — In electronic commerce, when an individual places an order and purchases the items he or she had previously selected.

contributing set — The set of privacy policy rules that make up the privacy policy advocated by a policy resource.

data descriptor — One part of a data element; the 'name' portion of the name-value pair.

data element — A single data value and its associated descriptor (i.e., a name-value pair).

data value — One part of a data element; the 'value' portion of the name-value pair.

dependency diagram — A UML diagram illustrating the dependencies between modules of the software. The arrows point from a module to the module(s) on which it depends.

e-commerce	"Commercial activity conducted via electronic media, especially on the Internet; the sector of the economy engaged in such activity" [1].
e-economy	Economy based on the wide use of information, knowledge and technology. It includes things like e-health, e-commerce, e-banking, and e-government.
electronic commerce	See *e-commerce*.
enterprise	A large business organization spanning multiple countries, comprised of smaller organizations called *retailers* or *businesses*.
enterprise privacy policy	The privacy standards that an enterprise determines for itself based on an analysis of the privacy obligations that might apply to them.
entity	Anything that exists as a discrete unit; for example, an individual, an application, or a business.
filter	A software module in the J2EE specification intended to allow for pre-processing of user-submitted HTTP requests sent to a J2EE-compliant application [111].
framework	A set of assumptions, properties, concepts, and values that constitute a way of viewing reality.
HTML	HyperText Markup Language; an authoring language used to express documents on the World Wide Web
HTTP	HyperText Transfer Protocol; an Internet protocol for transferring files. HTTPs is the same protocol, but transmitted securely.
information flow	A set of data elements that are sent from one entity to another.
interface	In Java, an abstract type which is used to specify an interface (in the generic sense of the term) that Java classes must implement [126].

OECD	Organisation for Economic Cooperation and Development, an organization of 30 member countries that share a commitment to the digital economy. Through its active relationships with other countries, NGOs and civil society, it encourages the growth of the digital economy by publishing internationally agreed instruments, decisions and recommendations in areas where multilateral agreement is necessary [92].
PIA	See *privacy impact assessment*.
policy resources	Entities that have some authority over, or influence on, enterprise privacy policies.
policy rule	The most basic building block of a privacy policy; a single element. E.g., 'Do not collect a social insurance number.'
POST	An encoding of user-submitted information in an HTTP request.
privacy impact assessment	"A process to determine the impacts ... on an individual's privacy and ways to mitigate or avoid any adverse effects" [117].
product specification	"An agreement among the software development team [defining] the product they are creating, detailing what it will be, how it will act, what it will do, and what it won't do" [94].
retailer	A business involved in electronic commerce.
set of policy resources	The set of all entities that have some authority over, or influence on, an enterprise's privacy policies.
software error	When the software does something, or does not do something, in such a way that it deviates from the product specification.

TRUSTe	A non-profit organization founded in 1997 to certify and monitor web site privacy policies, monitor practices, and resolve consumer privacy problems [119].
UML	A specification that helps specify, visualize, and document models of software systems, including their structure and design [86].
validation	The process confirming that a software product meets the user's requirements [94]
verification	The process of confirming that software meets its product specification [94]
workflow	"The operational aspect of a work procedure: how tasks are structured, who performs them, what their relative order is, how they are synchronized, how information flows to support the tasks, and how tasks are being tracked" [129].
XML	eXtensible Markup Language; allows designers to create their own customized tags, enabling the definition, transmission, validation, and interpretation of data between applications and between organizations.
XSLT	A language for translating an XML document into other text-based documents, including plain text files, HTML, or XML documents with different structure [135].

Acknowledgements

Isaac Newton once said, "If I have seen a little further, it is by standing on the shoulders of giants." I'm no Isaac Newton, but the same is true for me. This work would not have been possible without the assistance of many wonderful people.

First, thanks to my three supervisors who provided help and guidance the whole way through developing and writing my dissertation. Thanks to Kelly Lyons' urging, I actually started writing before I was done implementing, a singular achievement. Mike McAllister helped me discover the joys of LaTeX and submitted helpful and witty revisions, often on very short notice. And Jacob Slonim, after patiently helping me find my way, kept up a sustained flood of revisions for several months. I sincerely thank each of you. Thanks also to Carl Hartzman, who took the time to read and comment on my dissertation and offered insightful and probing questions at my defense.

I want to thank the IBM Centre for Advanced Studies (Toronto) for their funding and support. In particular, Kelly went above and beyond when she agreed to be one of my supervisors, and Jen Hawkins' dedication to her job, the CAS students, and her role as my RSM knows no equal.

Thanks to the employees of IBM who helped with my research and implementation, especially Darshanand Khusial. Also thanks to Terry Chu, Jack Wang, Jacob Vandergoot, and Ross McKegney, and many others.

My graduate work has also been funded by Precarn, NSERC, Symantec, and the Canadian Medical Association. Without them, I would not be able to both do my research and eat: two things I love very much.

My friends have supported me for years; I don't name you all here, but you know who you are.

Finally, I thank my family for their unfailing support. I may be standing on the shoulders of giants now, but you are the rock I've stood on all my life.

Chapter 1

Introduction

Privacy was once defined as the "right to be let alone" [20]. As new technology developed, this definition was extended to mean that individuals should have control over when and to whom they divulge personal information and what the recipient may do with the personal information upon receipt. Improved database management systems, distributed and federated databases, data mining algorithms, and software applications enable the collection, aggregation, sharing and use of a growing amount of information, but can also offer the specification of individual privacy preferences and better privacy protection and compliance verification.

Electronic commerce is becoming an important sector of the knowledge economy. Business revenue from electronic commerce has increased by 500 per cent from 2001 through 2005 in Canada, and experts predict continued increases until at least 2010 [109]. However, this growth is limited by the privacy, security and trust concerns of consumers. Consumers disclose their personal information online to businesses engaged in electronic commerce that they trust. These businesses, which often operate on the scale of enterprises, rely on consumers' agreement to disclose their personal information to enable payment and delivery; on the other hand, consumers rely on the enterprise collecting this personal information to protect it. In some countries, including Canada, enterprises are working to comply with legislation that protects personal information privacy.

In addition to consumer requirements and legislation, an enterprise will have privacy requirements based on the cost-benefit analysis of privacy protections, industry standards, its contracts with other enterprises, and the privacy policies of its competitors. From these requirements, an enterprise must determine its data handling practices, and in particular what measures it will take to protect the privacy of the information it collects, uses, stores, and shares. These practices are codified in an internal privacy policy.

Once an enterprise has created its internal policy on privacy, the policy is verified and approved before being deployed throughout the enterprise. Once the policy is deployed, the enterprise must ensure that its employees, business processes, and software comply with the policy. As the influences on the enterprise change, or as the enterprise changes (e.g., a merger or acquisition), so will its policy on privacy; the revised policy must again be implemented by the employees, business processes, and software applications. When revising its policy, the enterprise must either ensure that existing customers agree to the new policy or develop a mechanism to operate under both the original and the new policies. Given the quantity of information collected and the capabilities of electronic commerce software applications, verifying the compliance of software applications is a complex process.

This book begins by describing privacy as it relates to society, technology, e-commerce, and public opinion. Definitions, both modern and historical, provide context for the remainder of the discussion.

Second, this work presents an incremental approach with two major parts to the methodology. First, we informally describe an enterprise privacy policy management framework. This framework enables the process of determining enterprise privacy policy based on the influence of factors from both outside and inside the enterprise, validating and verifying this privacy policy, deploying and enforcing this privacy policy, and testing employees, business processes, and software applications for compliance with this written privacy policy. We define the properties and requirements of the actors and modules of this framework. Finally, we define the enterprise privacy requirements and design a software framework for a software application capable of managing enterprise privacy policy.

Third, we develop a proof-of-concept implementation for two modules of the framework: the privacy policy creation module, and the privacy compliance testing module. To create policy, we define the set of influences on an enterprise privacy policy as a set of policy resources. We define the properties of policy resources, of the privacy policies preferred by the policy resources, and of the privacy policy rules that comprise each privacy policy. We describe a means of consistently representing the policies in a manner suitable for information processing. Using this representation, we present a methodology for automatically determining which privacy policy elements should be contained within the enterprise privacy policy.

To demonstrate the viability of creating policy using this incremental approach, we implement proof-of-concept policy creation that represents two of the most important policy resources (legislation and the internal constraints of the enterprise) and from them define a sample privacy policy for an enterprise.

To test for compliance with the privacy policy, we propose a privacy compliance testing methodology for testing software applications that does not require modifying the original software application. This methodology builds a model of the flows of personal information as it passes through the access and exit points of the software application and stores this model in an information flow report. The access and exit points are identified from the workflow diagrams. The personal information is described using a set of data labels which are defined based on the data descriptors assigned by the software application. The flows of personal information are compared to a set of rules and flows detected as being non-compliant with these rules are recorded in the information flow report as either a warning or an error. The contents of the report are translated into different views based on the intended user. The information flow report is recorded in an XML-based language that we defined for the purpose.

To demonstrate the feasibility of the framework, we develop a proof-of-concept implementation for a leading electronic commerce software application, in cooperation with the software vendor. This provides realistic data and a realistic environment for our proof-of-concept. We test a sample e-commerce retailer store for compliance with a sample set of rules we defined in policy creation implementation.

The framework and each of the implemented modules are designed for incremental enhancement. The proof-of-concept implementation is extensible to include additional detail and functionality as the framework is built upon in future work. This work describes the core framework and tests for compliance with using a sample set of rules.

The remainder of this book is organized as follows. Chapter 2 describes the background and the state-of-the-art in privacy as it relates to electronic commerce, policy, and technology. Chapter 3 presents the research hypotheses and defines the overall framework for enterprise privacy policy management, including the process of determining the factors affecting an internal policy on privacy, from them creating computer-readable privacy policy rules, and testing software for compliance with these rules. Chapter 4 describes the implementation and results of a proof-of concept analysis that determines a privacy policy from two influences and of a proof-of-concept software application that implements the privacy compliance testing methodology. A discussion of the hypotheses, results, contributions, and future work is provided in Chapter 5.

Chapter 2

Background and Related Work

Privacy is a multi-faceted issue. Individual perspectives define it, laws enforce it, enterprises define it in their policies, and software engineers write software that protects or infringes upon it. This chapter introduces and defines privacy, examines privacy standards and privacy in legislation, addresses privacy in electronic commerce, and discusses the effect that technology has on privacy and vice versa.

2.1 Privacy and the Knowledge Economy

Privacy is a legal consideration for electronic commerce (e-commerce) [90], electronic banking (e-banking) [25], electronic health records (e-health) [105], and electronic government services (e-government) [91]. A Canadian law protecting the privacy of personal information collected by the private sector took effect in January 2004 [7], and other countries have passed similar laws to protect privacy (e.g., the European Union member states) [42]. The media discusses privacy during reports on identity theft and large security breaches, making the public more aware of privacy issues [51]. Since 1999, books like O'Harrow's "No Place to Hide" [89], Garfinkel's "Database Nation" [50], and Brin's "The Transparent Society" [21] have discussed the erosion of privacy in what they call the Information Age.

Privacy is not a new issue. In 1890, after the invention of the camera, Warren and Justice Brandeis published a paper in the Harvard Law Review [20] asserting every individual's right to privacy. In 1967, with the advent of large centralized databases, Alan Westin discussed information and privacy in his book "Privacy and Freedom" [121]. In 1974, as the electronic record-keeping abilities of the United States government increased, the federal government acquiesced to public demands for legislation governing the storage and use of personal information by the federal government and passed the *Privacy Act* [4]. The pattern is reactive: as technological developments challenge the previous definitions of "privacy", individuals, businesses, and legislators react with updated definitions designed to ensure a level of privacy equivalent to the level before the technological developments. Redefinitions can be major (as with the advent of large electronic databases) or minor (as businesses invent new ways to make use of the information stored in large electronic databases). The legislation follows behind the new technology [26].

Agre and Rotenberg [10], in their introduction to "Technology and Privacy", discuss the shifts in the relationship between privacy and technology since the 1980's:

> Tectonic shifts in the technical, economic, and policy domains have brought us to a new landscape that is more variegated , more dangerous, and more hopeful than before. These shifts include the emergence of digital communications networks on a global scale; emerging technologies for protecting communications and personal identity; new digital media that support a wide range of social relationships; a generation of technologically sophisticated privacy activists; a growing body of practical experience in developing and applying data protection laws; and the rapid globalization of manufacturing, culture, and the policy process...

There is no universal view on privacy. Groups like Privacy International and the Electronic Privacy Information Center assert that privacy is an inviolable human right and that legislators must protect it [42]. Another perspective or point of few can be summarized by Scott McNeally of Sun Microsystems: "You have zero privacy anyway. Get over it" [106]. A third point of view is that privacy is a value, like morality, and the government ensures each individual has the freedom to make his or her own choices [53]. The point of view or perspective of each individual may be different, as described in more detail in Section 2.1.3.

2.1.1 Definitions of privacy

The Oxford English Dictionary defines privacy as follows:

> a. The state or condition of being withdrawn from the society of others, or from public interest; seclusion.

b. The state or condition of being alone, undisturbed, or free from public attention, as a matter of choice or right; freedom from interference or intrusion... [2]

When Warren and Justice Brandeis wrote about privacy in 1890, they defined it as "the right to be let alone" [20]. This definition of privacy is cited as a defense against wiretaps, surveillance, and unreasonable arrest or detainment.

When computers and networks became capable of storing and transferring large amounts of information, raw data about individuals became a commodity that could be collected and easily sold or traded in large quantities [10]. With the new ability to collect and retain information, and the possibility of additional uses for this information, the definition of privacy took on another dimension. Alan Westin recognized this in 1967, defining privacy as "...the claim of individuals...to determine for themselves when, how, and to what extent information about them is communicated to others" [121]. In 1991, Bruce Phillips, the Privacy Commissioner of Canada, addressed the changing definition of privacy as follows:

> Justice Brandeis, in his famous 1898 [sic] definition of privacy as "the right to be let alone", could not have contemplated a world of ingenious machines with unlimited capacity for collecting, collating, and transmitting information across global networks... The right to be left entirely alone, if it ever existed, could now be exercised, if at all, only in the farthest corner of the most remote reaches of our arctic...
>
> But if absolute privacy in modern society is neither attainable, practical, nor even particularly desirable, the struggle must continue to preserve the individual's right to decide the degree to which personal privacy is to be sacrificed on behalf of other competing rights and claims. [98]

The Privacy Commissioner of Canada uses "the right to control access to oneself and to personal information about oneself" as a modern definition of privacy [99]. Federal legislation in Canada [7] defines Canadians' privacy rights in more detail, listing 10 core principles based on the Canadian Standards Association's model code [24] (see Section 2.1.2). Agre and Rotenberg also noted the shift in privacy definitions

(Section 2.1) and defined privacy as "the capacity to negotiate social relationships by controlling access to personal information" [10]. The definition of privacy in the information age, as used in this book, includes keeping personal information confidential and providing a mechanism to ensure the individual has control of their personal information.

2.1.1.1 Personal information

Personal information is broadly defined by Canadian legislation as "information about an identifiable individual" [7]. It does not provide examples of personal information. The California Information Practices Act lists the following items as examples of personal information [107]:

1. Name

2. Social security number

3. Physical description

4. Home address and home telephone number

5. Education

6. Financial matters

7. Medical or employment history

8. Statements made by, or attributed to, the individual.

Our research uses the preceding definition for the terms *personal information*. The same definition is used for the terms *personally identifiable information*, and *personal data*. The term *information* refers to both personal and non-personal information.

2.1.1.2 Confidentiality

The International Standards Organization (ISO) defines *confidentiality* as "ensuring that information is accessible only to those authorized to have access" [71]. It states that if an individual reveals personal information to an entity, that entity must reveal the information only to those the individual has authorized to view it.

The notion of confidentiality is well-established in sectors of the economy that deal with sensitive personal information. Hospitals and doctors have a duty of confidentiality regarding their patients' personal health information [23], a principle that is codified in the Hippocratic Oath [125]. Any information revealed by an individual to an attorney is protected by confidentiality laws [128]. In Canada, academic records are kept confidential and not made available to third parties (e.g., [88]).

These confidentiality principles must be upheld by technology in the information age.

2.1.2 Privacy in legislation

The Canadian private sector is governed by the *Personal Information Protection and Electronic Documents Act (PIPEDA)* [7], which applies to any private sector organization executing commercial transactions. *PIPEDA* requires that private sector organizations meet 10 core principles, which we summarize as follows [7]:

1. *Accountability*: An organization must designate an individual or individuals as accountable to the consumer for the organization's privacy compliance.

2. *Identifying Purposes*: When collecting personal information, an organization must identify the purpose of collecting this information.

3. *Consent*: An organization must have the knowledge and consent of the individual before collecting, using, or disclosing personal information.

4. *Limiting Collection*: An organization should collect only the personal information necessary for the purpose for which it is collected.

5. *Limiting Use, Disclosure, and Retention*: Once personal information is collected for a stated purpose, it shall not be used or disclosed for reasons outside of that purpose, and should not be retained for longer than is needed for that purpose.

6. *Accuracy*: Personal information should be accurate and up-to-date.

7. *Safeguards*: Personal information shall be protected to the extent necessary, relative to its sensitivity.

8. *Openness*: Personal information management policies should be made available to individuals.

9. *Individual Access*: Upon request, an individual must be told about any information the organization is storing, what it is being used for and to whom it is being disclosed, and shall be able to view the stored information and, if necessary, challenge its accuracy.

10. *Challenging Compliance*: Individuals must have a contact individual or individuals to whom they can address concerns about an organization's compliance with these principles.

These core principles were adapted from the Canadian Standards Associations's model code [24], which was based on the Organisation for Economic Co-operation and Development (OECD) Guidelines on the Protection of Privacy published in 1980 [90]. Canada is a member country of the OECD.

The Canadian public sector has been governed by the *Privacy Act* [8] since 1983. It requires that federal government departments and agencies limit the collection, storage and use of personal information, and provides for individual access to and correction of personal information stored by a government agency.

All of the provinces and territories have their own privacy or access to information legislation [36], though the content of these laws varies. As of 2006, British Columbia, Alberta, Ontario, and Quebec have passed provincial legislation deemed 'substantially similar' to *PIPEDA*, so the private sector in those provinces is held to the provincial law and not to *PIPEDA* [87].

The United States has specific legislation protecting specific types of personal information or groups of people (for example, video rental records are protected (*Video Privacy Protection Act* [5]), as is the information of children under the age of 13 while online (*Children's Online Privacy Protection Act* [6]). There is no federal law broadly addressing the privacy of personal information held by corporations. The Graham-Leach-Bliley Act governs information handled by the financial sector of the economy, and the Health Insurance Portability and Accountability Act governs information handled by the medical sector of the economy. There is a federal law regulating the government's use of personal information, the *Privacy Act* [4] of 1974. There are a number of state-level laws protecting the privacy of personal information collected and/or stored by corporations. For example, California has passed laws addressing identify theft, security breaches, and privacy online [22]. New York has had the Internet Security and Privacy Act [108] since 2002.

The resulting variance in state laws across the United States is the stated explanation for why large corporations like Microsoft have begun advocating for a federal privacy law in the United States [84].

The European Union Data Protection Directive [45], passed by the European Parliament in 1995, sets a standard of privacy for digital data processing in member countries of the European Union. Other directives, such as the 2002 Directive on privacy and electronic communications [46], set additional standards for the privacy of electronic communications. As of April 2006, all twenty-five member countries had passed national privacy laws compliant with the Data Protection Directive [44].

The OECD Guidelines and the Data Protection Directive are similar to the Canadian legislation. Table 2.1 shows the common elements among the Guidelines, the Data Protection Directive [45], and the Canadian Standards Association Model Code for the Protection of Personal Information [24] as found in the Personal Information Protection and Electronic Documents Act [7].

Privacy law must evolve as new technologies are developed. In February 2006, the Center for Democracy and Technology in the United States reported that "information and communications technologies are changing so rapidly that they are outpacing the law's privacy protection" [26]. They cite United States Supreme Court Justice Stephen Breyer as saying "advancing technology has made the protective effects of present law uncertain, unpredictable, and incomplete." The report concludes that lawmakers must revise legislation to meet the advances of technology.

Privacy legislation in eighty countries is covered in detail by the Electronic Privacy Information Center and Privacy International in their report on "Privacy and Human Rights" [42].

	Principle	OECD [90]	EU [45]	Canada [7]
1	Accountability	✓		✓
2	Identifying Purposes	✓	✓	✓
3	Consent	✓	✓[1]	✓
4	Limiting collection		✓[2]	✓
5	Limiting use, disclosure, retention	✓	✓	✓
6	Accuracy	✓	✓	✓
7	Safeguards	✓	✓	✓
8	Openness	✓		✓
9	Individual access	✓	✓	✓
10	Challenging compliance	✓	✓	✓

Table 2.1: Comparison of the OECD Guidelines on the Protection of Privacy [90], the European Union's Data Protection Directive [45], and the Canadian Standards Association Model Code for the Protection of Personal Information [24] as found in PIPEDA [7].

2.1.3 Privacy and public opinion

There are privacy laws and privacy definitions (see Sections 2.1.2 and 2.1.1 for more detail), but these representations do not capture the details of privacy. They represent a common denominator or a norm of privacy principles.

One aspect not captured is the individual nature of privacy. Public opinion polls show that individuals' opinions on privacy vary [55]. Culnan and Armstrong [34] reported in 1999 that individual perspectives on privacy varied, though when presented with a binary decision individuals would categorize themselves as being either concerned about privacy or not concerned about privacy. An individual's preferences will be influenced by factors including recent news reports about privacy [51], age and geography [101], education [13], pre-existing levels of trust [101], and the stated practices of a given enterprise [34, 101]. An individual's views on privacy may change over time as the influencing factors evolve. Thus, individuals' privacy views are personal, variable, and dynamic. Alan Westin has published nine privacy surveys since 1978. The results were collected by Kumaraguru and Cranor and reported in 2005 [78], and are summarized in Figure 2.1. The percentage of respondents who were "very

---
[1] Merged with principle 2
[2] Merged with principle 5

concerned" about their personal privacy almost doubled between 1978 and 1999. The percentage who were "very" or "somewhat" concerned held steady in the early 1990's, but increased slightly by the end of the decade. By 1983, five years after the first survey, the percentage "very concerned" had increased by 27% to 49%.

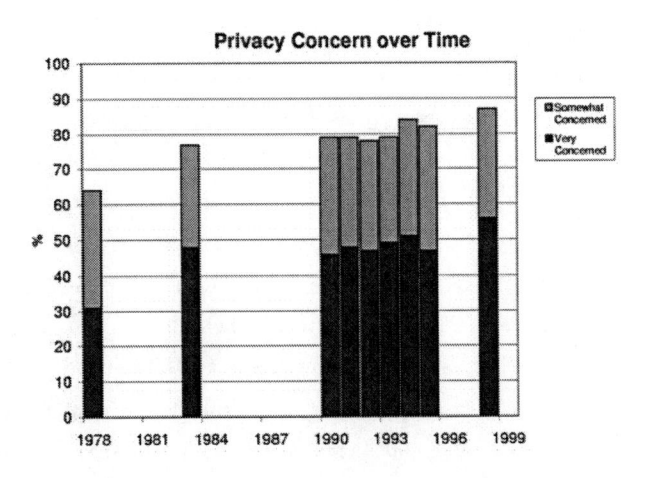

Figure 2.1: General privacy concern since 1978 (data from [78]).

There are international, language, and cultural aspects to privacy. Internationally, laws and public opinion differ [42]. Milberg et al. established in 1995 that the levels of concern about privacy varied among the nine countries they surveyed [85]. Culturally, Westin stated in 1967 that concern for privacy is expressed differently in different cultures [121]. Milberg also reported that cultural factors (as defined by Hofstede [57]) were correlated with whether or not the government was pressured by its citizens to adopt privacy regulations [85]. Hofstede's cultural factors included power distance (a measure of the power wielded by powerful members of the society over less powerful members), individualism versus. collectivism (how important the individual is versus how important the group is), masculinity versus. femininity (to what extent "traditional" gender roles were assigned in the society), uncertainty avoidance (how much value the society places on things being predictable), and long- versus short-term orientation (to what extent the society plans for the future) [57].

Kumaraguru and Cranor [77] studied attitudes toward privacy in a sample of well-educated, urban-dwelling individuals working for outsourcing companies in India. Figure 2.2 reproduces their comparison of their study to a previous study of American Internet users. The most noticeable difference is that general concern for privacy is relatively lower compared to the American numbers (concern for privacy on the Internet in particular is equivalent). When asked about personal comfort with providing personal information online, the Indian individuals were more likely to be comfortable providing personal information such as age, income, and medical history than Americans were (although concern about sharing email addresses was the same). They also reported higher levels of trust for businesses and governments. Structured interviews found that common practices such as posting university grades on notice boards or online (a practice made illegal in the United States by the Family Educational Rights and Privacy Act (FERPA) [3]) did not elicit significant concern about privacy from those surveyed. The report explains the differences between American and Indian perspectives on privacy by the presence of two separate cultures, but does not establish more detailed reasoning. The report explains the similarities by pointing to the spread of the Internet and increased communication between the United States and India.

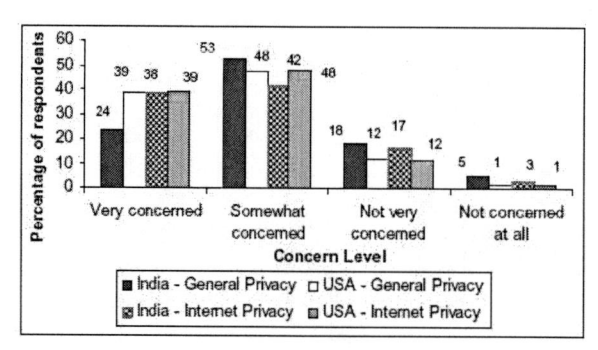

Figure 2.2: General and Internet privacy concern in India, compared with 1998 survey of American Internet users (reproduced from [77]).

Altman defined privacy as an exercise in managing the boundaries between private space and public space, where the boundary is a shifting line that depends on the context and the intent of the entity requesting access to an individual's private space (where the private space includes any type of personal information) [11]. He believed that 'privacy' could not be represented using static definitions.

Privacy concerns vary by sector of the economy. Public opinion polls in 2000 showed that a consumer's trust varies based on who he or she is dealing with (e.g., 96% trust nurses, whereas 31% trust casino owners) [96]. Privacy requirements for electronic health and initiatives to meet them (see Choy and Goldman's 2001 study in [28]) are different from the requirements and initiatives for electronic commerce (see the legislation described in Section 2.1.2 and chapter 3 of the book by Bahadur, Chan, and Weber [16]). This work approaches privacy in the electronic commerce sector, but our general framework is designed to be applicable or adaptable to the other sectors of the economy.

2.2 Commerce, Privacy, and Policy

2.2.1 The e-economy

Industry Canada defines the e-economy as "the use of information and communications technologies for product and process innovation across all sectors of the economy" [70]. An e-economy is created by leveraging information and communications technology (ICT) to transform organizations and business processes to be competitive and innovative. The e-economy is said to be a "revolution" with as much impact as the introduction of steam, electrical, and fossil fuel power centuries ago [70]. A major impact of this "revolution" is that more interactions are conducted electronically, usually through the Internet. This "revolution" has been called the *knowledge revolution* [115], and the e-economy has been called the *knowledge economy* [37].

The e-economy includes a broad category of interactions conducted using ICT. Industry Canada (2004) [70] and Amor's "E-business (R)Evolution" (2001) [12] mention the following subcategories:

- *e-health*: health care offered via or augmented by ICT (e.g., telehealth or electronic health records).

- *e-government*: government services offered through ICT (e.g., online tax form submission, online census).

- *e-learning*: education offered via or augmented by ICT (e.g., online courses, distance learning over the world wide web).

- *e-business/e-commerce*: commercial activity conducted via electronic media [1], including but not limited to:

    - *business-to-consumer e-commerce (B2C)*: commercial activity between businesses and consumers conducted via electronic media (e.g., "online shopping")
    - *business-to-business e-commerce (B2B)*: commercial activity between businesses conducted via electronic media
    - *enterprise-to-enterprise e-commerce (E2E)*: commercial activity between enterprises conducted via electronic media
    - *e-auctioning*: auctions conducted electronically (e.g., eBay)
    - *e-banking*: conducting bank transactions electronically. This usually refers to consumer-to-bank and not bank-to-bank (e.g., online banking)
    - *e-gambling*: gambling conducted electronically
    - *e-trading*: buying and selling stocks electronically

Each of these subcategories has privacy implications; however, this book focuses on business-to-consumer e-commerce or e-business, which will be referred to as *e-commerce*.

2.2.2 Electronic commerce

Electronic Commerce, or e-commerce, is the general term for "commercial activity conducted via electronic media, especially on the Internet" [1]. This general term refers both to businesses selling directly to consumers (B2C) and businesses engaging in online commercial activity with other businesses (B2B). This research focuses on the business-to-consumer model of electronic commerce, but for simplicity refers to it as electronic commerce or e-commerce.

In Canada, revenue from e-commerce increased by 500% from 2001 through 2005 (Figure 2.3) [109]. In 2005, 36% of that revenue was from business to consumer sales

[109]. Analysts at Forrester Research predict that e-commerce revenue will grow by another 15% each year until 2010, when it will account for 13% of North American retail sales [72]. Electronic commerce is growing and will continue to grow. As e-commerce grows, so does the number of individuals disclosing personal information and the number of businesses collecting, storing, and manipulating this electronic information. Privacy concerns regarding e-commerce should be addressed.

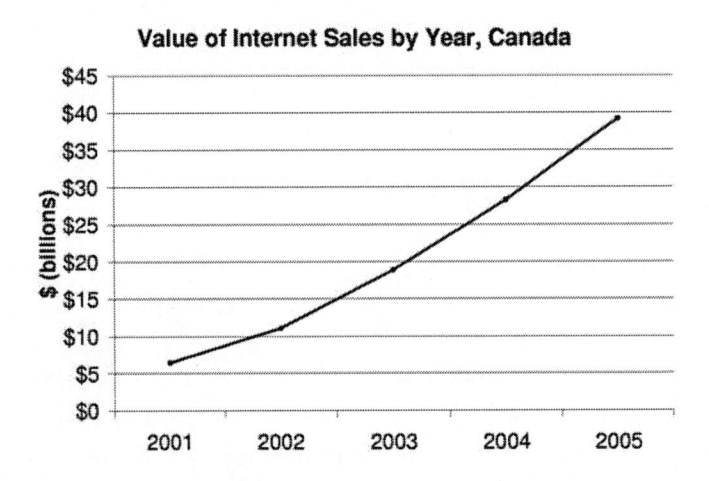

Figure 2.3: Value of Internet Sales in Canada from 2001-2005 (data from [109])

The principal stakeholders in an e-commerce transaction are shown in Figure 2.4, and include the **customer**, the **regulators**, and the **enterprise** (the enterprise is the business, and sub-contracts tasks such as delivery services). The customer is an individual who interacts with the e-commerce store. Over the course of their interaction (as represented by commerce workflow diagrams), they may browse a store catalog, register with the store, add items to a shopping cart, place an order ("check out"), or other actions depending on the business (e.g., Figure 2.5). A retailer is one store (or in general, a subset) of the many that belong to the enterprise that operates the online store, with the primary goal of selling goods (physically or electronically) and/or services. The regulators includes legislators, government agencies, voluntary privacy seal programs (see Section 2.3.1.3 for details), the enterprise itself, standards bodies, and other entities that regulate e-commerce. A fourth stakeholder not visible in Figure 2.4 is the e-commerce **software vendor**. According to Forrester Research,

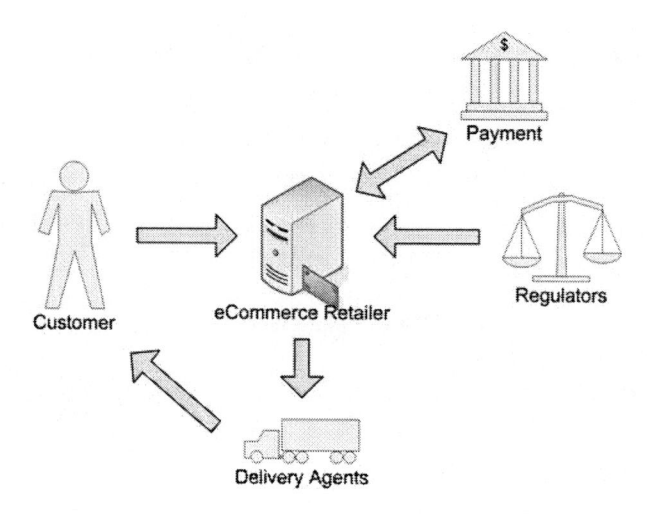

Figure 2.4: A set of interactions in an e-commerce transaction: ordering, payment, delivery, all governed by a set of regulations.

37% of North American and European online businesses will purchase or upgrade e-commerce software from a software vendor in 2006 [83]. The software vendor develops this e-commerce software, which is also governed by the regulators. Figure 2.6 shows the high-level view of these four stakeholders.

2.2.3 e-Commerce stakeholders' privacy views and requirements

Each of the stakeholders described in the previous section has a view and/or a set of requirements regarding privacy. Some have privacy obligations to other stakeholders. This section looks at the views and requirements of the four primary stakeholders. **Customers** which choose to reveal personal information to businesses online receive benefits such as the ability to make purchases on credit [33] and home delivery. When disclosing this personal information, customers have privacy, security, and trust concerns. According to a 2002 study by Harris Interactive, some are so concerned about privacy that they do not participate in e-commerce (26%); a majority are concerned, but willing to provide personal information if necessary (64%), and 10% have no privacy concerns about sharing personal information online [55]. A survey conducted by the United States Federal Trade Commission (FTC) found that 92% of consumers

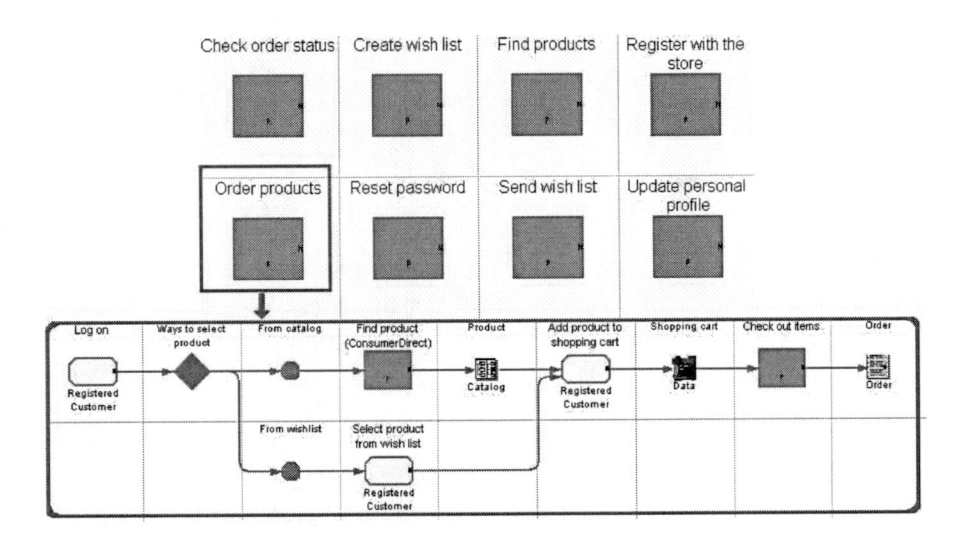

Figure 2.5: WebSphere Commerce workflow diagram for the shopping workflow and the order product sub-workflow [65].

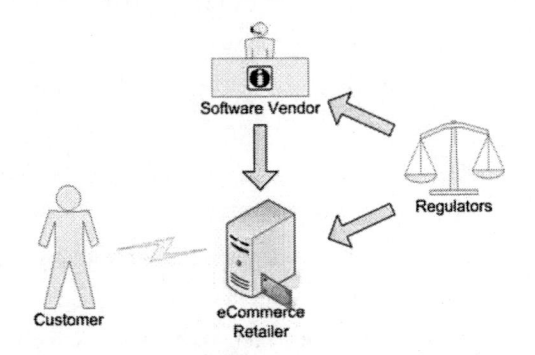

Figure 2.6: The high-level view of the main stakeholders in an e-commerce B2C model.

are "very concerned" or "concerned" about the misuse of their personal information online [48]. A Jupiter Media Matrix report issued in June 2002 puts the number of online consumers who were "worried" about privacy at 70% [74]. A Harris Interactive survey found that the most significant consumer concerns regarding personal information security online were companies trading personal data without permission, the consequences of insecure transactions, and theft of personal data [54]. The theft of personal data (identity theft) is a relatively new concern - the United States Department of Justice reported in April 2006 that 3.6 million American households were victims of identity theft in 2004, 6% of them more than once [17]. Actual financial losses were reported in 70% of the cases, it took days or weeks to resolve the issue, and 25% were still experiencing problems a year later [17].

Businesses and enterprises have to meet and balance a variety of privacy requirements from different sources, including their customers, relevant legislation, data-sharing contracts, and industry standards. Section 3.2 addresses this enterprise privacy policy formulation process in more detail. For the business, legal requirements may be the most critical.

According to the Customer Respect Group, the current state of privacy protection by online businesses is "worrisome" [35]. In 2005, they studied corporate privacy policies as posted online. When they examined policies regarding sharing collected personal data, they rated 42% of the policies as "good" [35]. When they examined policies regarding re-using personal data for marketing, they rated 72% as "poor" [35]. One area where they reported improvement was written privacy policies - they rated 64% of privacy policies as "good" for their clarity [35]. These ratings are subjective, although they can still provide an indication of relative quality and trends over time.

Businesses have positive incentives to meet consumer privacy standards. A PriceWaterhouseCoopers consumer study in 2000 reported that almost two thirds of those polled "would shop more online if they knew retail sites would not do anything with their personal information" [38]. A 2002 Jupiter Research study estimated that "on-line retail sales would be approximately twenty-four percent higher in 2006 if consumers' fears about privacy and security were addressed effectively" [74].

E-Commerce Software vendors' privacy concerns are driven by the demands of their customers (the enterprises and/or retailers) and the potential of legal liability for providing software that violates privacy laws. A well-publicized privacy violation by a business using a software vendor's product might damage the reputation of the software vendor and cause other enterprises to obtain software elsewhere or develop it in-house. The privacy-protection requirement is an aspect of desired software functionality and needs to be tested for compliance (see Section 2.3.2 for more on software testing and Section 3.2.5 for more on privacy compliance testing).

Regulators create privacy regulations. The issues they regulate are influenced by a number of factors including consumer demands. Privacy regulation is addressed in more detail in Section 2.1.2.

2.2.4 Privacy non-compliance consequences for e-commerce enterprises

The enterprise conducting business online and the software vendor may each encounter consequences if caught violating privacy requirements. As of April 2006, these potential consequences apply in the western world.

- Fines: Violating privacy laws may result in fines. In 2004, Universal Music Group (UMG) Recordings paid $400,000 in penalties for collecting and using the personal information of children under the age of 13 [49], a violation of United States law. In Canada, the maximum fine for a PIPEDA violation is $100,000 [7].

- Restrictions on marketing or operations: DoubleClick, an online marketing company, built profiles of the online behavior of thousands of Internet users. When they proposed a merger with a company that would give them the ability to uniquely identify the individual to whom the profile applied, consumer advocates and governments launched an investigation into the potential for invasion of privacy. Part of the eventual settlement included mandatory expiry dates on DoubleClick's advertising cookies, independent privacy audits, a re-write of their privacy policy, a periodic purge of personal profiles, and better opt-out notification and user education [29]. These restrictions were imposed even though Doubleclick eventually settled the cases against them with the FTC and the states' attorneys general.

- Decreased stock value: Public controversy can negatively impact stock value. In the DoubleClick case, its stock was worth about $135 per share in January 2000. After the lawsuits and investigations were launched, the share price dropped to $30 per share, even before the so called "dot-com bubble burst" [114].

- Civil settlements: In the DoubleClick case, DoubleClick paid over $1.8 million in damages and investigation costs [29].

- Cost of Investigations: Responding to complaints from consumers or from privacy commissioners requires time and resources. The court may order that the business pay for the investigation costs ($450,000 from DoubleClick, for example) [29].

- Recurring investigations and privacy audits: The UMG Recordings case mentioned above required UMG Recordings to submit to an annual audit every year for three years [49].

- Bad publicity: The fines and civil settlements, when covered by the media, can generate consumer dissatisfaction and mistrust. Consumers may not do business with the business, which will result in decreased revenue. Although the effect of public privacy breaches on consumer confidence has not been systematically studied, a 2004 Accenture study found that 51% of consumers will avoid doing business with companies they do not trust [116].

- Loss of contract: If a contract stipulates data handling practices and a business violates these practices, they may be in breach of contract and lose the contract, pay a penalty, or both. In 2005, it was revealed that CardSystems, a credit card processing company, had stored 40 million credit card numbers in violation of its contracts, and further had left the stored numbers vulnerable to a security breach. Visa and American Express revoked CardSystems' ability to process credit cards [19].

2.2.5 IBM® WebSphere® Commerce

Software vendors are included as e-commerce stakeholders since a privacy violation involving their applications could be damaging, and an estimated 37% of online businesses will purchase or upgrade e-commerce software packages in 2006 [83]. One major e-commerce software vendor is IBM with the WebSphere Commerce product [63]. According to independent studies by Forrester Research [82] and Gartner Research [102], IBM is the leader in the Business-to-Business market and one of the two leaders in the Business-to-Consumer market. (The other is Art Technology Group's ATG Commerce [15].) In this section, some details of the WebSphere Commerce product are described. In later chapters, WebSphere Commerce is the e-commerce application around which our proof-of-concept implementation of privacy compliance testing is built.

WebSphere Commerce is a software solution for businesses engaged in e-commerce. It is an end-to-end solution for e-commerce that allows for extensive customization. Several sample e-commerce stores are shipped with the application, but it is most commonly used as a 'toolbox' containing implementations of business processes common in e-commerce (e.g., user registration, payment authorization, catalog management). These implementations can be assembled and customized into online stores. It can be used for B2B, B2C, or E2E e-commerce; this research studies it in only the B2C context.

WebSphere Commerce is a Java application running on WebSphere Application Server™ (WAS), an implementation of the Java Enterprise Edition (J2EE) platform specification [112]. WebSphere Commerce and WAS are offerings of the IBM WebSphere software family. WebSphere Commerce uses servlets to do server-side processing for specific tasks and Java beans to execute programming logic. Data is retrieved from and stored to a data source using Enterprise Java Beans (EJBs), which provide a layer of abstraction between the database and the application logic. Information is presented to the user using different views that can be generated using templates, called Java Servlet Pages (JSPs).

The Java classes that execute programming logic are called "commands". There are three major types of commands in WebSphere Commerce [64]:

1. **Controller commands**: Receive requests from a web controller, invoke task commands to execute specific logic, and forward the browser to a view command. Controller commands can be executed directly by visiting their URL in with a web browser. An example is the `UserRegistrationAddCmd` controller command, which receives user registration information and invokes task commands to store the user's information.

2. **Task commands**: Execute specific logic. These contain the implementation

of the logic desired from a controller command. An example is the `AuditUser RegistrationCmd` task command, which is invoked by the `UserRegistration AddCmd` to ensure the validity of the information submitted by the user.

3. **View commands**: Respond to requests by returning a "view": HTML, XML, or other web-based pages. An example is the `HttpForwardViewCommand` view command, which calls a Java Servlet Page (JSP) to produce a view based on a set of input parameters.

2.2.6 Business policy management

The meaning of the word 'policy' in this research is drawn from business policy in the context of information systems. Business experts define policy as a "statement of procedure or principle by which a company intends to realize its objectives" [136]. Maullo and Calo define it as "a set of considerations designed to guide decisions on courses of action" [80]. The Wikipedia article on policy defines it as "a plan of action to guide decisions and actions..." [127]. Policies in the context of information systems are "operating rules that can be referred to as a means of maintaining order, security, consistency, or other ways of successfully furthering a goal or mission" [122].

A business entity may have hundreds of policies (or more), though they may not be explicitly referred to as policies. Examples might be "customer service email response time must be less than 24 hours" or "corporate accounts have higher priority than personal accounts" [80]. This work refers to these policies as 'enterprise policies'. These policies will evolve and be implemented over time and must be enforced by employees and incorporated within the processes of the business [136]. Section 3.2 addresses the formulation of enterprise privacy policies in more detail.

Business entities defining explicit policies practice some form of policy management. According to Maullo and Calo, "Policy management deals with the establishment, communication, maintenance and execution of enterprise information processing policies... it spans a wide spectrum of organizational activity, from the high level goals conceived by human intelligence, to the sets of management tasks executed by computer automation" [80]. Policy management adds structure and process to the task of creating, deploying, and enforcing enterprise policies. The policy management process includes the identification of different alternatives and choosing among them on the basis of the impact they will have and the justification for having the policy. Policy management in the context of privacy policy is described in more detail in Section 3.2.

2.2.6.1 Policy and privacy

The business policies of the previous section may include an enterprise privacy policy, which is part of the internal data management practices the enterprise intends to follow.

The term "privacy policy" is used to refer to a notice placed on a website informing customers about how the operator of a website deals with personal information [123], and sites that handle personal information have a link to a written privacy policy [35, 47, 48]. This is the consumer view of a privacy policy and differs from the internal policy adopted by an enterprise.

This work will refer to a privacy policy as an internal enterprise privacy policy that expresses the privacy practices the enterprise intends to follow.

2.2.7 Privacy impact assessments

The Treasury Board of Canada defines a privacy impact assessment (PIA) as "a process to determine the impacts ... on an individual's privacy and ways to mitigate or avoid any adverse effects" [117]. The office of the privacy commissioner of New Zealand defines it as "a process whereby a conscious and systematic effort is made to assess the privacy impacts of options that may be open in regard to a proposal" [110]. An organization may use a PIA to assess their internal privacy practices and identify areas for improvement.

The Chief Information Officer (CIO) of the Treasury Board of Canada Secretariat published a Privacy Impact Assessment Policy [118] and an accompanying set of guidelines [117] in 2002 that apply to all government bodies subject to Canada's *Privacy Act* [8]. The guidelines identify a number of "best practices" for privacy impact assessments, which are generalized here to the following points:

- Determine the scope of the PIA, including what business units of the organization it will cover, what privacy standards or policies will be enforced, and who will be completing the assessment. This step may be completed by the organization's CIO and the remaining steps delegated to the appropriate teams within the organization.

- Determine the flow of data through the business unit. Business process diagrams are a useful starting point and can be expanded into the detailed data flows required.

- Analyze the data flows in the context of relevant privacy policies. For each of the data flows or business processes, complete a questionnaire that examines the activity in light of the requirements imposed by legislation or other obligations. Identify activities that place personal information at risk of exposure or that do not comply with the privacy policies. The guidelines present a basic questionnaire with 100 questions as a starting point. The content of the questionnaire may vary depending on the business unit in question.

- Document the areas that present the greatest risk of violating the privacy policies and suggest appropriate remedial action.

A Privacy Impact Assessment is a tool recommended by privacy commissioners to ensure an organization's business processes respect individual privacy and, where applicable, comply with privacy legislation (e.g., [100, 110]). A PIA is conducted regularly to ensure continued compliance. Additional assessments may be required if new privacy policies are imposed, a privacy policy violation is discovered, new business processes are created, new software is installed, or new projects are initiated.

A PIA does not ensure that the personnel and software that implement the business process are actually complying with the written policies. It is a manual self-assessment process where the answers are obtained and entered manually. In-house tools may be developed to simplify completing the questionnaires, reporting the results, and tracking progress over time.

2.3 Technology and Privacy

Technology can be one of the causes of privacy violations, but can also be part of the solution. New technologies present privacy challenges, but technology can also be leveraged to increase available privacy protection. The following sections describe technologies that can enhance privacy protections online.

2.3.1 Privacy enhancing technologies in e-commerce

Privacy Enhancing Technologies (PETs) are described in five parts: we begin with a discussion of the Platform for Privacy Preferences, list some types of privacy software tools for consumers, describe privacy seal programs, provide an overview of the Enterprise Privacy Authorization Language, and list privacy software tools and privacy services for enterprises.

2.3.1.1 Platform for privacy preferences (P3P)

Operators of web sites may publish a privacy policy describing their handling of personal information (see Section 2.2.6.1). Another way to express a privacy policy is a machine-readable privacy policy as specified by the Platform for Privacy Preferences (P3P) [133]. P3P is based on the eXtensible Markup Language (XML) [132]. The first version of specification (1.0) was issued by the World Wide Web Consortium (W3C) in April 2002 [130].

A P3P policy states the purpose for the collection of data, the access consumers have to their own personal information, the choices consumers have with regards to personal information usage, and the remedies available if the privacy policy is violated. It does not provide enforcement or provide protection for a consumer's personal information; it allows software applications to help individuals manage their privacy based on the privacy promises of businesses [32]. P3P does not replace human-readable policies; the P3P specification requires a URL referencing a human readable policy and also requires that the two policies be consistent.

The following are the main elements in a P3P policy. Further details of the P3P specification are available from the W3C [130].

1. `<ENTITY>`: Describes the organization that controls or owns the site. It uses the P3P data schema to represent this information.

2. `<ACCESS>`: Indicates what access a consumer has to their own personal information once it is stored by the web site operator. The pre-defined values range from `<none/>` - no access is permitted to `<all/>` - all identifiable information is accessible.

3. `<DISPUTES>` - Outlines the recourses available to the consumer if the site does not abide by its policy. There may be more than one dispute resolution method. This section will also list what remedies are available from a pre-defined set.

4. `<STATEMENT>`: the core of the policy. There may be multiple statement elements. This element specifies the data collection practices of the site. This component may contain the `<NON-IDENTIFIABLE>` tag to indicate no identifiable information is collected. Otherwise, the following elements will be present:

    (a) `<CONSEQUENCE>`: A plain-text explanation of how the consumer benefits from this data practice.

    (b) `<PURPOSE>`: One or more of twelve pre-defined elements explaining what the information will be used for. A generic element is included for purposes that don't fall under the other eleven elements.

    (c) `<RECIPIENT>`: One or more of six elements characterizing the types of organizations that will have access to the information. Organizations are grouped based on their data protection practices ranging from `<ours/>` (the business and its agents) to `<unrelated/>` (third parties whose practices are unknown to the business).

    (d) `<RETENTION>`: An element describing for how long the site retains the personal data; the pre-defined values range from `<no-retention/>` to `<indefinitely/>`.

    (e) `<DATA-GROUP>`, `<DATA>`: the The `<DATA-GROUP>` element contains `<DATA>` elements that specify what information is gathered from the consumer. The type of data gathered is specified in the mandatory 'ref' attribute.

The attribute 'optional' specifies whether this information is required to access a resource or complete a transaction. This value will typically be one of the elements in the P3P base data schema, but can also be one of the elements in a customized data schema. <DATA> elements can include a <CATEGORIES> element containing one or more of the 17 P3P categories to better indicate what this information will be used for.

The P3P base data schema is a pre-defined set of the most commonly collected elements of personal information. It is divided into four subsets: computer information (e.g., IP address), personal information (e.g., address), business information (e.g., job title), and third-party information (e.g., information provided about one's spouse). The base data schema can be extended to include other data elements.

As of May 2006, the next version of the P3P specification (1.1) is in the last call of the public working draft stage [131]. P3P 1.1 can be applied to XML documents and allows sites to specify recipients of personal information by jurisdiction. The major change in P3P 1.1 is the format for specifying base data schema, which is now done using an XML Schema Definition [131].

Reception of P3P has been mixed, and adoption as of 2003 was still limited, four years after the publication of the P3P specification in 1999.

Online consumer advocacy group Center for Democracy and Technology and the Privacy Commissioner of Ontario support the adoption of P3P, stating that it helps consumers manage the privacy of their personal information [27]. Microsoft Corporation included features that make use of P3P in Internet Explorer version 6.0.

Consumer advocacy group the Electronic Privacy Information Center (EPIC) and Karen Coyle of Computer Professionals for Social Responsibility are critical of P3P [31, 39]. EPIC asserts that P3P is "complex and confusing". They point out that "good" web sites may be penalized for not deploying a P3P policy while sites with inferior privacy policies are rewarded. They believe that P3P does do not allow for expressive policies that accurately capture a site's privacy practices.

Giles Hogben from the European Commissions's Joint Research Centre (JRC) recognizes P3P's shortcomings but has a plan to address them. He published a list of P3P shortcomings and their possible solutions, based on their implementation of P3P

1.0 in their P3P Proxy application [73]. He identifies issues including the vocabulary used to describe security precautions, the inability to verify that claims in the policy regarding obtaining consent are true, the base data schema, and the inability to enforce P3P policies on the enterprise [73]. As one of the authors of P3P 1.1, he is advocating changes to address these issues

In November 2003, Byers et al. reported that 21% of the 500 most-visited websites (according to Netscore) and 12% of a random sample had posted P3P policies. One third of the deployed policies had syntax errors and did not comply with the P3P specification.

2.3.1.2 Privacy software tools for consumers

The Electronic Privacy Information Center [41] maintains a list of privacy-enhancing tools and services for consumers [40]. The (non-exhaustive) list includes the following categories:

- **Snoop Proof Email** tools offer methods of encrypting emails or accessing email through the web using Secure Socket Layers.

- **Anonymous Remailers** allow individuals to create multiple anonymous email addresses that all forward to a single email account. This allows them to send and receive email anonymously.

- **Surf Anonymously** tools offer the ability to browse the world wide web anonymously or pseudo-nonymously. This functionality is offered through proxy servers that obscure an individual's IP address, block cookies, remove banner advertisements, and re-write Javascript code.

- **HTML Filters** are client-side software tools that prevent web browsers from downloading banner advertisements, pop-ups, and other forms of online advertising.

- **Cookie Busters** manage or block cookies placed on an individual's computer by a web site.

- **Voice Privacy** tools offer encrypted voice-over-IP solutions.

- **Email and File Privacy** tools encrypt or password protect files and emails.

- **Secure Instant Messaging** offer encrypted instant messaging, including text-based and video-chat instant messaging.

- **Telnet Encryption** software uses Secure SHell (SSH) to encrypt information sent using the Telnet protocol.

- **Disk Encryption** tools encrypt a user's entire hard drive.

- **Disk/File Erasing Programs** completely erase files so that they cannot be recovered or undeleted. The normal delete operation removes only the reference to data, but does not delete the data itself (a "soft delete"). These tools completely obliterate the data, a process which takes longer but is more secure (a "hard delete").

- **Privacy Policy Generators** help web site administrators generate privacy policies, either in plain-text or P3P (Section 2.3.1.1) format.

- **Password Security** tools help generate passwords that are difficult to guess and less susceptible to dictionary-based attacks.

- **Firewalls** restrict network access to (or from) an individual's computer.

2.3.1.3 Privacy seal programs

A privacy seal program is a voluntary self-regulation program to which an enterprise may subscribe if they agree to "high standards of personal information protection" [119]. The third-party organization offering the service (e.g., TRUSTe [119]) agrees to intervene on a consumer's behalf if the enterprise does not follow their stated privacy policy. The site is issued a graphic to place on their web site indicating that they are enrolled in this program.

Privacy seals had about 500 enrolled businesses by 2000, three years after the program began [48]. As of April 2006, 1800 businesses were enrolled with TRUSTe [95]. Goldman reported in 2003 that customers are not concerned about the presence or lack of a privacy seal [52]. A March 2006 survey conducted for TRUSTe found that 47% of respondents had heard of privacy seals and 15% said that the presence of a privacy seal affected their behavior "often" [95].

2.3.1.4 Enterprise privacy authorization language

The Enterprise Privacy Authorization Language (EPAL) is an XML-based language designed to codify data handling practices using detailed authorization policies, with the goal of enforcing an enterprise privacy policy [61]. Where P3P is designed to represent a set of promises to an enterprise's customers, EPAL is designed to specify the obligations and conditions to which stored information is subject.

An EPAL policy first lists the hierarchies of users, data, and purposes relevant to the enterprise, then defines sets of actions, obligations, and conditions (adapted from IBM's description [61]):

- user-categories: the entities (users or groups) that use collected data (e.g., technical support, marketing)

- data-categories: the categories of collected data that are handled differently from a privacy perspective (e.g., demographic-data, financial-records)

- purposes: the tasks for which the data is used (e.g., sending promotional material, aggregate statistics)

- actions: the actions on the data (e.g., published versus. modified)

- obligations: certain actions on the data that must be executed (e.g., delete after 30 days unless specifically given permission)

- conditions: Boolean expressions that evaluate the context (e.g., "the user-category must be an adult" or "the user-category must be the primary care physician of the data-subject")

EPAL was submitted to the W3C standards track by IBM in 2003, but as of April 2006 is not a W3C standard.

A drawback of EPAL is its focus on authorization and access control. It accurately expresses a policy on access control for information, where the access control is based on privacy requirements also expressed in EPAL. However, it does not represent important parts of an enterprise privacy policy, such as how consent is obtained, what information may be collected from a customer, and what information may be shared outside the organization.

2.3.1.5 Privacy software tools and services for enterprises

This study addresses privacy policy management and privacy compliance software testing for the enterprise. Products and services addressing privacy issues exist, and include:

- *Privacy impact assessments* and *external privacy audits*: Accounting and enterprise services firms are offering custom privacy impact assessments or privacy audits as a service. For example, Ernst&Young offers "Privacy Advisory Services" [43] and IBM Global Services offers a "privacy strategy and implementation" service for $50,000-$250,000 [69].

- *Privacy policy authoring*: Enterprises deploying P3P, EPAL, or plain-text privacy policies use tools to help the process. Examples include the IBM Tivoli Privacy Manager^{TM} (converts natural language policies to P3P and helps author EPAL policies) [66] and the OECD privacy policy generator (generates a natural-language privacy policy) [93].

- *Privacy policy enforcement*: The IBM Tivoli Privacy Manager [66] can convert EPAL documents (Section 2.3.1.4) into role-based access control policies that for compliance with the policy as expressed in EPAL.

- *Privacy management infrastructures*: This service includes suites of products marketed as encompassing solutions to privacy. The privacy protections are limited to providing access control and encryption solutions based on privacy policies. Examples include the Voltage "Enterprise Privacy Management Platform" [120] and the Primedius Digital Privacy "Business Protection Services" [97].

2.3.2 Software testing

Software testing is a part of the software life cycle, used to "identify the correctness, completeness and quality of developed computer software" [124]. It examines and exercises software in order to identify errors. This section is a brief introduction to some of the properties and terminology of software testing, especially those relevant to the privacy compliance testing described in later chapters.

An error in a software product occurs when the software does something that deviates from the product specification [76]. A product specification is "an agreement among the software development team [defining] the product they are creating, detailing what it will be, how it will act, what it will do, and what it won't do" [94]. *Verification* is the process of confirming that software meets its product specification [94].

Validation is the process confirming that a software product meets the user's requirements [94]. User requirements are the functions of a software product that the eventual user of the software product requires or expects. The product specification is generally derived from a user requirements document.

Patton [94] defines a number of software testing axioms, five of which are summarized here. The first is that it is *impossible to completely test a program*. There are too many possible inputs and too many possible outputs, and between them there are too many paths through the program. The second is that *software testing is a risk-based exercise*. Since it is intractable to test every aspect of the entire software project, certain parts of the program are chosen for testing. The untested portions may still contain errors, meaning they each present the risk that an error exists and will manifest itself once the software is in use. A balance needs to be struck between managing risk and expending too many resources exhaustively testing software. This risk-based view of software engineering is discussed further in Section 2.3.2.1. The third is that *testing will not prove errors do not exist*. It can find errors, but it cannot prove there are no errors. The fourth is that *errors come in groups*; the more errors detected in a software component, the more errors there are likely to be. The fifth is that the *software will eventually become 'immune' to tests* if the test strategy is never changed, but the errors will still exist.

Software must be tested for security. One of the early proponents of security testing is Beizer [18]. He identified a growing concern about ensuring software security, and discussed design and testing steps to increase the security. Like Patton [94], he reminds us that it is impossible to prove a software system is error-free. He states it is impossible to prove that a software system is totally secure. It is a risk-mitigation-based exercise (see Section 2.3.2.1), just like testing for privacy. Like privacy, security should pervade the entire software design process, and existing test methodologies should be used to ensure that security has not been compromised [18]. An approach to security testing is the creation of a security threat model, which is discussed in Section 2.3.3. Our approach to privacy compliance testing creates a model of the information collected and used by the software application.

2.3.2.1 Risk-based decisions

All software testing decisions are risk-based decisions [94]. In the testing domain, 'risk' is a frequently used term to denote the balance between the benefits and downfalls of two opposing options when a perfect solution is not available.

For example, the 'risk' a software error presents is assessed based on the probability that it will be detected, on the probability that it will cause problems, and on the severity of the problems it may cause (where the severity may be measured by the value of the loss or the cost of recovery). Based on the level of severity of error, a determination is made whether to fix the error, to postpone the fix, or to not fix it. If the decision is to not fix it or to postpone the fix, the developer assumes risk [94]. Microsoft development teams use a metric called DREAD to assess this risk [113] (Section 2.3.3 has details).

Another risk is taken when determining what to test. Testing each line of code at least once is not a complete test of a software application [18]. The test team must decide what parts of the code will be tested and which will not. The untested code presents a risk that there will be an error in that code, and that this error will manifest itself and do damage.

Risk is not limited to software errors. Decisions like assigning junior team members to test critical functionality can also present a risk [94]. In general, a "risk" is the possibility that a decision made while testing will turn out to be the wrong one.

In the context of privacy, a "privacy risk" is the possibility that an enterprise may mishandle personal information in such a way that one or more data handling privacy requirements are violated and adverse consequences result (Section 2.2.4). These requirements may be legal, contractual, consumer-based, and/or any other sources.

2.3.3 Security threat models

Security threat modeling does for security what our approach does automatically for privacy. One of the most commonly cited approaches to security threat modeling is Microsoft's approach. In their documentation [59, 81, 113], they present a structured approach to modeling targets and potential attacks, intended to aid in designing and testing software systems. Their recommended steps, adapted from their guide to threat models for web applications [81], are as follows:

1. *Identify Security Objectives.* Identify the goals and constraints relevant to your software and any data related to it. Determine the legal and contractual requirements, sensitive data in need of protection, and intangible assets in need of protection. These are high-level objects; for example, "Prevent malicious users from accessing customer information."

2. *Create an Application Overview.* Define the application, including its functions, users, properties, and data. This includes drawing the end-to-end deployment scenario, identifying the roles and privileges assigned to groups of users, listing examples of the most common uses of the application ("use cases"), determining what major technologies are manifest in the application, and identifying the key aspects of the application's security mechanisms.

3. *Decompose the Application.* Create a detailed view of the application's handling of data in three major categories:

    (a) Trust Boundaries: The areas where the level of trust changes, like from outside the software system to inside the software system, or between web pages for which authentication is required and web pages where authentication is not required.

   (b) Data Flows: The path information follows, from creation time to deletion time. The flow can be high-level (between an application and a database server) or low-level (transferred between two web pages).

   (c) Entry & Exit points: The components of an application that receive information from external sources, or that send information from external sources. (In this case, an external source is any entity outside of the application.)

4. *Identify Threats.* Determine what attacks or actions might be used by an attacker to violate the security objectives from Step 1. A starting point is a list of common software vulnerabilities (e.g., buffer overflows) and common attacks (e.g., SQL injection or dictionary attacks). A next step is to step through the use cases identified in Step 2 and determine what a malicious user might attempt to attack the system at each step. Finally, use the data flow details to identify threats at the exit and entry points and ways that a user might attempt to breach a trust boundary. Once an initial list of threats is compiled, the list is organized in a tree-like hierarchical structure. Recognizing patterns in this structure helps identify additional threats.

5. *Rate the Threats.* Threats are rated based on their risk, often according to this formula: $risk = probability\ of\ occurence * damage\ potential$. If a problem is likely to occur and will cause significant damage once it does, the threat gets a high rating. A more complex measure is the DREAD metric calculated as the sum of the scores assigned to **D**amage potential, **R**eproducibility, **E**xploitability, **A**ffected users, and **D**iscoverability.

6. *Identify Vulnerabilities.* Less relevant in the design phase of the software lifecycle, but in development or testing, determine which of the threats from Step 4 might result in a violation of the security objectives from Step 1, given the current implementation or design of the application. These threats should be documented thoroughly. Deal with each vulnerability in a way appropriate to the rating assigned in Step 5.

Once a threat model report is generated for the design of a software application, designers can integrate this threat model into the design process; developers can consult it and mitigate risk during development; and testers can use it as a basis for test cases or to ensure the implementation is adhering to decisions made during the threat modeling steps [59].

2.3.4 Privacy risk modeling for ubiquitous computer systems

The notion of a security threat model (Section 2.3.3) has been extended to the domain of privacy in ubiquitous computing by Hong et al. [58]. The authors discuss methods of assessing the privacy risk present in computer programs or advanced systems that track user's movements, location, actions, and the like (ubiquitous computing). They draw a direct parallel between what they call "privacy risk models" and "security threat models". The methodology proposed is very specific to the design of ubiquitous computing systems. It consists of a set of questionnaires designed to identify and manage the aspects of a ubiquitous computing system that present the risk of violating a user's privacy.

The set of questionnaires is an approach similar to the privacy impact assessments discussed in Section 2.2.7, and like the privacy impact assessments is manual, not automatic. When compared to the security threat models summarized in Section 2.3.3, this approach addresses steps 4 and 6 but does not have an equivalent for steps 1, 2, 3, or 5.

2.4 Summary

In this chapter, we provided a general introduction to privacy, a look at e-commerce and privacy, and a discussion of technology and privacy.

Our general introduction defined privacy and looked at the evolution of the definition from 1890, through the invention of large-scale databases, through to today. This book considers the privacy of personal information, and therefore defines privacy as "the right to control access to personal information about oneself". We described the privacy legislation in North America and Europe, and went on to discuss the aspects of privacy that make it difficult to define or legislate.

In our section on e-commerce and privacy, we described how electronic commerce was part of the e-economy before narrowing our focus to exclusively electronic commerce. We described the growth of e-commerce and continued by looking at the privacy views and obligations of four primary stakeholders in e-commerce, and the possible consequences of not meeting these obligations. We presented WebSphere Commerce, an e-commerce software application from IBM that we use in a later section to provide a real-world environment for our proof-of-concept implementation of privacy policy management. We discussed policy and what it means for enterprises before looking at an existing mechanism for testing compliance with privacy policies, a manual privacy impact assessment.

We began our discussion of technology and privacy by describing privacy-enhancing technologies. These included P3P, a set of consumer-oriented tools, EPAL, and a set of privacy policy compliance / privacy policy management tools and services available to an enterprise. We then described current software testing mechanisms and risk, an important aspect of software testing. We concluded by describing security threat models and a privacy risk modeling approach for ubiquitous computing.

Chapter 3

Methodology

This chapter begins by presenting two hypotheses and our methodology for verifying each of them. As part of the methodology we describe a framework for managing the privacy policies of an enterprise. The framework we describe will be developed incrementally. This research focuses on describing the first iteration which includes an informal description of the framework and a detailed description and proof-of-concept implementation of two modules in the privacy policy management framework. Each of the two modules corresponds to one of the hypotheses presented in the following section. This chapter concludes by describing the software requirements and a framework for enterprise privacy policy management.

3.1 Hypotheses

A retailer has incentive to determine what the influences on its privacy policy may be, determine what its privacy obligations are, define the privacy expectations of these influences and obligations, establish which of these expectations should comprise its privacy policy, and verify that its privacy practices comply with the established privacy policy. This research will address the following two hypotheses:

Hypothesis 1: *The entities that influence an e-commerce retailer's privacy policy can be identified, represented and used to determine the retailer's privacy policy as a set of structured privacy policy rules.*

Hypothesis 2: *It can be verified that the communications between an e-commerce retailer's software application and the retailer's consumers comply with a set of privacy policy rules.*

In particular, the first hypothesis is addressed by examining enterprise privacy policy. The enterprise's privacy policy is influenced by what we call the set of policy resources. The retailer is a subset of the enterprise and is therefore acted upon by a subset of the enterprise's influences as well as some retailer-specific influences, and the retailer's privacy policy is one of several privacy policies that together comprise the enterprise's privacy policies. We choose several exemplar influences, define their properties, uniformly represent them, combine them into a retailer's privacy policy, and translate them into a set of computer-readable rules. We additionally define a framework capable of representing, creating, and manipulating enterprise privacy policy. The methodology to follow all of this is described in Section 3.2.

We verify the second hypothesis by developing a proof-of-concept software implementation that examines the communications between the client (customer) and an electronic commerce software application, determines whether or not the information is personal, and reports on the compliance of each communication with respect to a pre-defined set of privacy rules. To verify the implementation, a real-world electronic commerce application is modified to generate communications that that do not comply with a sample enterprise privacy policy. The methodology is described in Section 3.2.5.

These hypotheses represent two modules of our overall approach to enterprise privacy policy management. Both our framework and these proof-of-concept implementations are designed to be incrementally extended as part of our iterative development process.

3.2 Enterprise Privacy Policies

An enterprise will create a set of privacy policies, each of which applies to a subset of the enterprise and is based on the influence exerted by the enterprise's stakeholders. These policies will be deployed and validated, and subsequently verified and enforced on the employees, processes, and software applications of the appropriate subset of the enterprise. After describing the framework for enterprise privacy policy management, we describe enterprise privacy policy management in four parts: (1) the set of policy resources, (2) the enterprise, its subsets, and how privacy policies are determined, (3) the resultant privacy policies, and (4) the deployment, enforcement, validation, and verification of the resultant privacy policies.

3.2.1 Enterprise privacy policy management

The role of enterprise privacy policy management (Figure 3.1b) in an enterprise is to create a privacy policy based on the influence exerted by the enterprise's stakeholders (Figure 3.1a) and then deploy and enforce this policy on the employees, processes, and software applications of the enterprise (Figure 3.1c,d,e). The following sections describe a methodology for creating a framework for privacy policy management (Section 3.2.1.1) of enterprise privacy policies drawn from policy resources (Section 3.2.3).

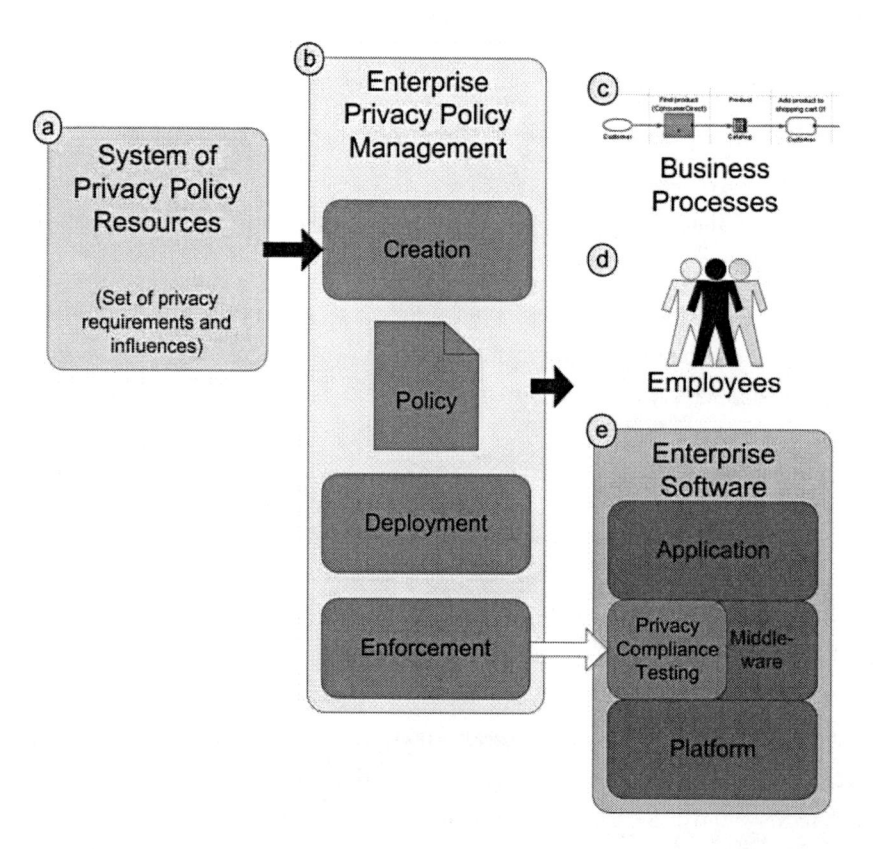

Figure 3.1: An overall view of enterprise privacy policy management.

3.2.1.1 Requirements of a privacy policy management framework

We start with the properties, assumptions and requirements of an enterprise privacy policy management framework, and of the software tools that would implement it. Here, we define *framework* as a set of assumptions, properties, concepts, and values that constitute a way of viewing the management of policy resources and policy enforcement / compliance testing.

1. **Component Representation.** The framework must encapsulate and be capable of representing the properties of the set of policy resources, the properties of the policy resources, and the properties of the privacy policies advocated by each policy resource. It must also be capable of modeling the interactions or mappings between them.

2. **Persuasive Consistency.** The privacy policies produced should be consistent, including:

   - External Consistency: The procedure for comparing privacy policies should be the same between two different sets of policies.
   - Internal Consistency: The results across the different privacy policy rules must be consistent. For example, if one element states "access must be provided" and another states "access must not be provided", only one can be true.
   - Consistency rule: Privacy policies should be interpreted similarly at different times, in different periods, and in different languages unless the circumstances have changed significantly.

3. **Identifiable Ambiguity.** The framework may not be capable of perfectly representing the policy advocated by a particular policy resource. In such cases, a determination must be made as to what policy item was not properly represented. Ambiguity may exist when a privacy policy can be understood more than one way by a reasonable person.

4. **Usable.** The non-technical employees and customers of the enterprise must be capable of competently interacting with the portions of the software with which

they must interface.

5. **Localization.** An international enterprise will draw policy rules from many countries. These policy rules will be in many languages; therefore, the framework must be capable of dealing with policies regardless of the language. Localization is the process of mapping a privacy policy to a particular language, culture, or domain within a country.

6. **Scalable.** Privacy policies and privacy rules will change in size or configuration to meet the needs of the changing environments (for example, in a peer-to-peer environment the software application must be capable of operating while considering a larger number of entities). Software applications attempting to build an enterprise privacy policy based on the set of policy resources and privacy rules must be capable of representing any number of policy resources and any number of privacy rules.

7. **Reliability.** Privacy policy management is an ongoing issue; the software must perform when needed and as required.

8. **Maintainability.** The software and rules must be easily extended, expanded, or updated to match changes in the process of determining enterprise privacy policy.

3.2.1.2 Framework for enterprise privacy policy management

Figure 3.2 shows the framework for enterprise privacy policy management software. The Enterprise Privacy Policy Manager (2) is the coordinator of the privacy management software. It retrieves privacy policies from the set of policy resources (1) and invokes the policy creation module (3) to combine the separate policies into one central enterprise privacy policy (as described in Section 3.2.3). The Manager further controls the execution of the framework after creation. The policy is deployed (4) to the enterprise, a process which includes publishing the policy, and updating business processes. The process is controlled by the Manager. The policy is maintained (5) by another module; this module controls updates and revisions to the policy, in coordination with the policy creation module. Another module enforces the policy

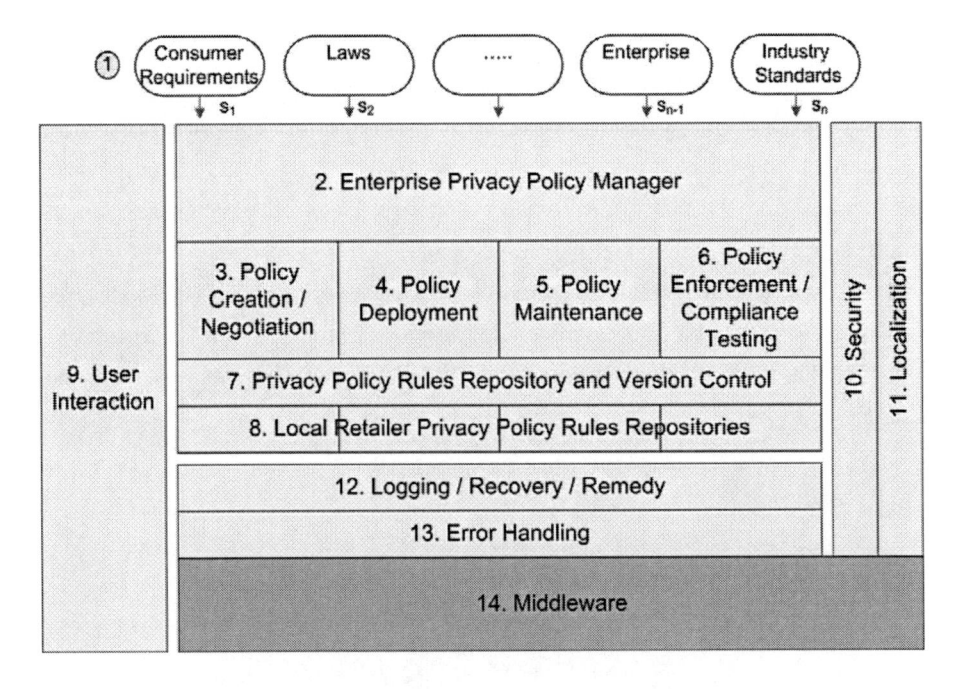

Figure 3.2: The enterprise privacy policy management framework.

and tests for compliance (6) (as described in Section 3.2.5.2 and Chapter 4). A final module is a policy repository (7) that the Manager and the other modules use to store and retrieve enterprise policies; it is also responsible for version control. This policy repository stores the policies of the entire enterprise and of each subset of the enterprise (called *retailers*). There is also a local policy repository at each retailer (8) which stores the privacy policy rules for that retailer and for the retailers with which it shares information. The manager and these modules are the central portion of the framework.

Proof-of-concept implementations of the policy creation module (3) and the policy compliance testing module (6) are included in this iteration of development to validate the feasibility of the framework.

A user interaction layer (9) is provided to manage interactions with the user. Generally, the user will be the system administrator or an employee of the enterprise. In some cases, the user will be the customer; for example, when testing for compliance, if a certain interaction with the customer does not comply with the privacy policy, the customer will be contacted by a module of the framework. The security layer (10) manages authentication and access control to ensure that only authorized individuals are modifying enterprise privacy policies. The localization (11) layer provides the manager and the modules with the means to work in other languages and to translate privacy rules from and to other languages, as well as to map rules from one language or locality to existing rules in other languages or localities. The logging/recovery/remedy (12) and error handling (13) layers log activity within the framework and take remedial action when errors occur. This framework operates just above the middleware layer (14).

3.2.2 Set of policy resources

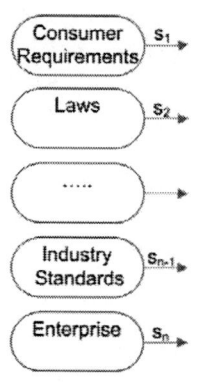

Figure 3.3: Policy resources that influence enterprise privacy policies.

An enterprise privacy policy is based on the preferred standards of a number of different groups that have influence on the enterprise. We call these entities *policy resources*. For a large enterprise, these policy resources will include, for example, existing enterprise privacy policy, requests of senior corporate officers (e.g., Chief Information Officer) or the board of the corporation, legal requirements, contractual requirements, consumer preferences, technological limitations, and industry standards (which may be *de facto* standards). Any number of policy resources may contribute to an enterprise's privacy policy. Collectively, these policy resources comprise the *set* of policy resources. See Figure 3.3 for a set of policy resources S, labelled $s_1, \cdots, s_n$. The following sections describe some of the properties of the set of policy resources and its components. In this informal description, we do not guarantee every possible property is represented; the list of properties can be extended in future iterations. New properties can be added as the framework matures and stabilizes over time.

3.2.2.1 Properties of the set of policy resources

The set of policy resources (Figure 3.4a) has the following properties:

1. **Interactive / Dependent.** Each policy resource can influence or exert authority over not only enterprise privacy policies, but other policy resources. For example, consumers might influence lawmakers to write new privacy laws. Principles codified in legislation may affect the data-handling requirements in contracts. Thus, each of the policy resources depends on and interacts with the other policy resources.

2. **Dynamic.** Policy resources will change over time. The set of policies they advocate or the strength of their influence relative to other policy resources may change. They may adjust independently, or they may change because of revisions introduced by the enterprise or other policy resources. For example, new legislation would change the statutory requirements. The enterprise moving to a new market segment could change the consumer policy resource or the industry standards / domain-specific policy resource. The enterprise entering a new country could change the legal policy resource or the consumer policy resource. Policy resources may be added to or removed from the set. The representation of the set of policy resources is required to be capable of representing any number of policy resources.

3.2.2.2 Properties of a policy resource

A policy resource (Figure 3.4b) consists of one or more privacy policies (Figure 3.4c) and a set of properties.

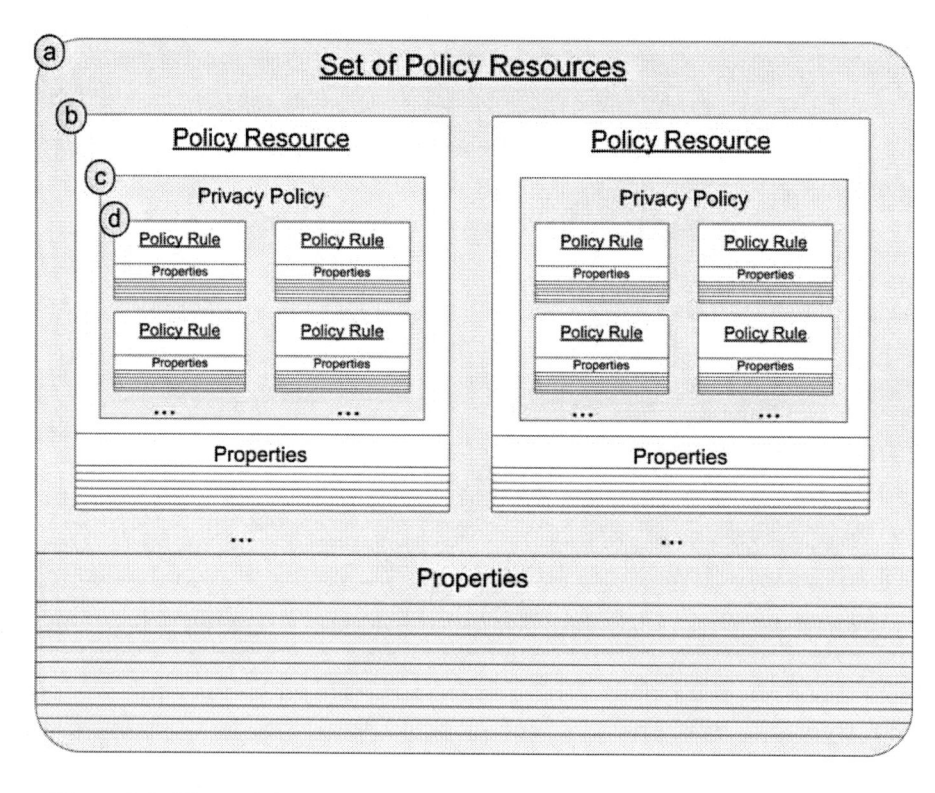

Figure 3.4: The set of policy resources (a), containing policy resources (b) which contain privacy policies (c) comprised of privacy policy rules (d).

The privacy policy consists of the privacy practices which the policy resource desires that the enterprise implement. The policy resources privacy policy, like the enterprise privacy policy, is a set of policy rules (Figure 3.4d). A policy rule is an individual privacy element, and is the most basic building block of a privacy policy. This privacy policy may be referred to as a *contributing set*. A policy resource and its privacy policy has the following properties:

1. **Policy resource name.** This property describes the policy resource (e.g., "consumer preferences" or "legal").

2. **Weight.** Some policy resources are more critical or important than others.

Importance, and therefore the weighting, may be assessed based on the consequences of disregarding the standards advocated by a particular policy resource. Any determination of an enterprise privacy policy based on the policy resources is required to take into account the relative weighting of each policy resource. For example, a statutory requirement may be weighted higher than a consumer preference and on par with a contractual requirement. A conceptual formula for calculating the weight is:

$$weight(force) = (relative\ importance\ of\ policy\ resource) + (relative\ penalty\ for\ violating\ requirements) - (relative\ cost\ of\ implementing\ requirements)^1$$

When the enterprise determines the weights assigned to each policy rule, the weights must be normalized relative to each other.

3. **Locality.** If applicable, the countries / regions / provinces / states in which this policy resource is relevant.

4. **Language.** The natural language(s) used by this policy resource.

5. **Version.** The version of this representation of the policy resource.

6. **Description.** A plain-language description of this policy resource, possibly written in more than one language.

3.2.2.3 Properties of a policy rule

A policy rule (Figure 3.4d) is an individual privacy rule, and is the most basic building block of policy resource privacy policies (Figure 3.4c) and the enterprise privacy policy. It has the following properties:

1. **Policy rule identifier.** This property uniquely identifies the policy rule using a two-part name - the combination of the originating policy resource name and a randomly generated unique integer string.

---

[1]The term 'relative' indicates that the weight matters only relative to other policy resources. Hence, the actual values in the formula should be normalized against the values of the other policy resources. The recommended normalization is to divide each weight by the max(weight).

2. **Weight.** Each individual policy rule in the contributing set of a given policy resource has a weight, just as the policy resource itself has a weight. This weight measures the importance of enforcing this rule to the given policy resource, relative to the other policy rules in the set. For example, the policy resource 'consumer preferences' might suggest ten policy rules, but the most important would be "do not ask for a social insurance number". The weight depends on the credibility, which is a measure of how much authority, believability, and relevance the source of that policy rule has to the enterprise. When the enterprise determines the weights assigned to each policy rule, the weights must be normalized relative to each other.

3. **Originator.** This property tracks from where the rule originated within this policy resource. It is not the same as a "source"; all policy rules in the enterprise privacy policy that are from the same policy resource will have the same primary source. However, the policy rules in a given policy resource will not necessarily share the same originator. For example, an originator in the "legal" policy resource might be the name of a privacy law. For the "contract" policy resource, the originator might be a unique identifier for the contract from which the rule is drawn.

4. **Description.** A plain-language description of the policy rule, possibly in more than one language.

3.2.2.4 Policy resources

We identify exemplar policy resources that typify the policy resources that influence an enterprise, in this case based on the model of a single electronic commerce retailer. In practice, the privacy policy of each retailer will be influenced by its own set of policy resources where the influence the policy resources have on the retailer differ from the influence present for other retailers. These exemplar policy resources are shown in Figure 3.5 and described in this section. One level of detail is given for each policy resource. There is likely to be overlap between different policy resources (Figure 3.6). The different policy resources are as follows:

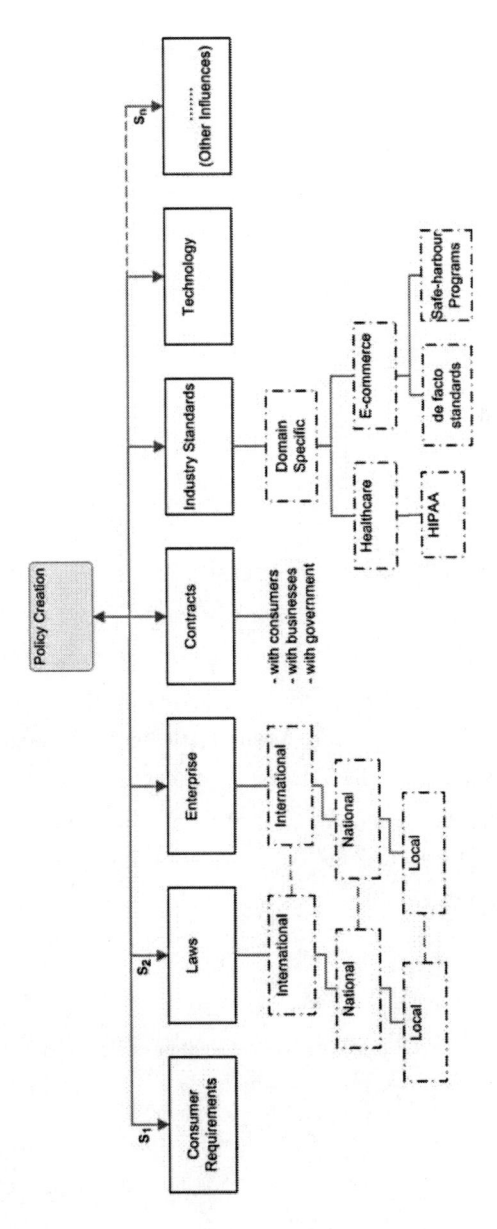

Figure 3.5: Exemplar policy resources and how they can influence enterprise privacy policies.

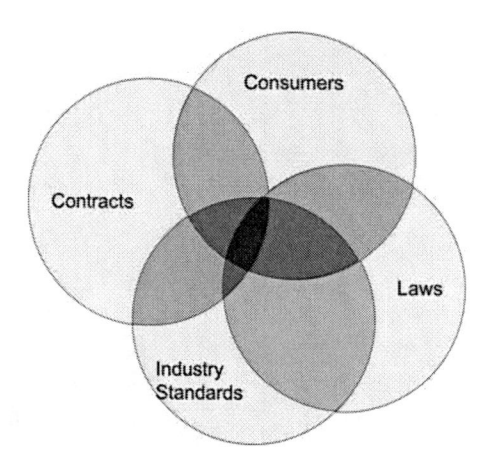

Figure 3.6: The overlap of four sample contributing sets.

- **Legal:** the laws to which the enterprise is subject in various operating jurisdictions. It consists of a collection of rules and consequences for violating these rules. These rules may be international laws, national laws, or local (state, provincial, municipal) laws, each with varying applicability to the enterprise's operation. Legal sanctions from former settlements or charges that require certain privacy practices to be followed are also part of the legal policy resource. This policy resource is illustrated in Figure 3.5 and Figure 3.7. Legal obligations will typically be heavily weighted as laws are enforceable and may carry significant consequences.

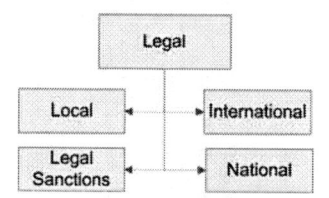

Figure 3.7: Components of the exemplar 'laws' policy resource.

- **Enterprise:** the internal constraints and forces that operate from within an enterprise to affect the resultant enterprise privacy policy, as well as any pre-existing enterprise privacy policy. The following are examples of internal forces that might impact the privacy policy; see Figure 3.5 and Figure 3.8:

- Enterprises may have `Chief Privacy Officers` who have broad authority to determine enterprise privacy policy [60]. This officer's personal views or experiences may affect the policy rules that are chosen. The same may be said for other corporate officers, but the Chief Privacy Officer has particular responsibilities regarding privacy policy. These responsibilities include (modified from the Federal Computer Weekly [56]):
    * Represent the enterprise, not individual citizens.
    * Teach the fundamentals of fair information practices.
    * Monitor compliance with privacy laws.
    * Assist with development of impact assessments.
    * Advocate privacy, remember security.
- `Competitors` have privacy policies, and the *de facto* standard set by these competitors will be an influence. Competitor policies may also affect consumer expectations if their policies allow consumers to expect a certain level of privacy protection.
- `Existing policy rules` may be expensive and time-consuming to replace; the enterprise may not wish to discard existing policy or may favour new policy rules that are similar to existing policy. For example, if an enterprise is required to give consumers access to their personal information when stored by the enterprise, they may choose to remain with the previous way of doing it (by written request sent via post) rather than implementing a web-based access method.
- The enterprise will consider `cost versus reward` when determining what policy rules are important. If the penalty for violating a rule is insignificant, implementing it may not be economically justifiable.

- **Consumer Requirements:** Consumer opinions of privacy in e-commerce (as stakeholders in e-commerce) are presented in Section 2.2.3 and may vary according to the different aspects of privacy discussed in Section 2.1.3. Customers, and potential new customers, will have expectations and requirements about

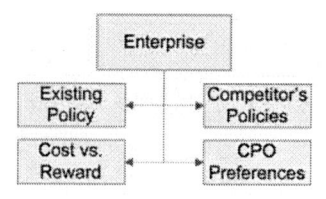

Figure 3.8: Components of the exemplar 'enterprise' policy resource.

how their personal information is handled. These requirements are impacted by the popular media. They differ from country to country. Consumers also have different requirements depending on the domain - they protect their health information more than their demographic information, but have more trust for a hospital using e-health than for a business using e-commerce [101]. An enterprise might use polling data, user studies, or customer surveys to determine what privacy policy will satisfy the greatest number of consumers at the lowest cost. This policy resource is illustrated in Figure 3.5 and Figure 3.9.

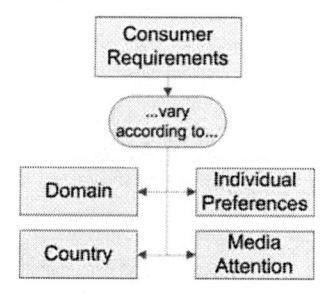

Figure 3.9: Components of the exemplar 'consumer requirements' policy resource.

- **Industry Standards:** Each industry or domain application will have its own standards that vary in nature, enforcement, and applicability. There are some international data management standards to which enterprises may choose to adhere or be required to adhere. For example, the ISO IEC 17799 [71] defines security standards for information. The Hippocratic Oath [125] says (translated from Greek) "All that may come to my knowledge in the exercise of my profession... I will keep secret and will never reveal." This policy resource is illustrated in Figure 3.5 and Figure 3.10.

Some countries or regions have signed cross-border flow of information agreements that govern the flow of information between them. For example, an enterprise operating out of Australia but wishing to share information with a subsidiary in Canada will need to follow the cross-border agreement signed between Canada and Australia. The Organisation for Economic Cooperation and Development (OECD) has defined guidelines for the protection of privacy [90] that an international enterprise may choose to use as guidelines.

The industry standards policy resource provides domain-specific policies and requirements in addition to the domain-specific policy inherent in the legal, enterprise, and other policy resources. Some of the policies that apply to e-health might be drawn from the American Medical Associations privacy code. Policies that apply to e-commerce might be based on the *de facto* standard. (A *de facto* standard is one that exists because it is widely used or widely accepted by a group of companies, but is not ratified by any official standards body (e.g., ISO). An example *de facto* standard is that retailers publish a page describing their privacy policy. These pages became a common fixture on websites after the United States Federal Trade Commission released a report calling for self-regulation [47, 48], even though nothing was mandated by law.)

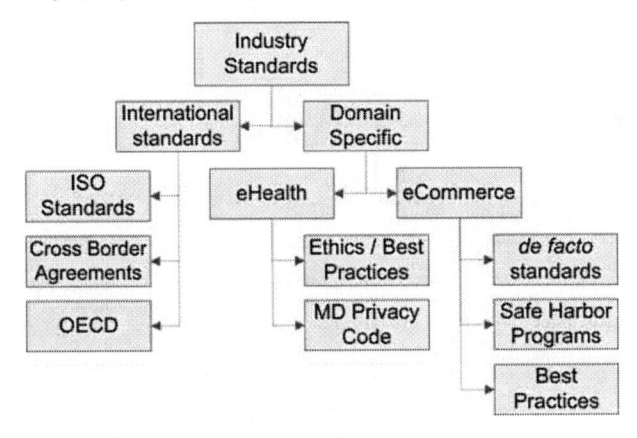

Figure 3.10: Components of the exemplar 'industry standards' policy resource.

- **Contracts:** Enterprises may have contractual obligations requiring a certain privacy policy. A contract with the government may require that information provided by the government not be used for any purposes other than those stipulated in the contract and never be revealed outside the enterprise or the person to whom the information pertains (for example, a social insurance number collected for tax purposes). A contract with consumers may be as simple as a website privacy policy to which the consumer agreed and to which the enterprise is required to adhere. Enterprises may also have contracts with other enterprises that outline the conditions of their information sharing. This policy resource is illustrated in Figure 3.5 and Figure 3.11.

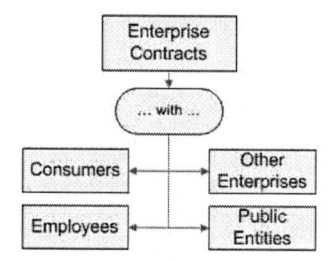

Figure 3.11: Components of the exemplar 'contracts' policy resource.

3.2.3 The enterprise and policy creation

Figure 3.12 shows the enterprise as a collection of retailers, from Retailer 1 to Retailer m. Each retailer comprising the enterprise is affected by a variable combination of the policy resources described in Section 3.2.2 ($s_1, s_2, \cdots, s_n$). For example, Retailer 1 is affected by s_2 and s_n (privacy laws and the enterprise itself according to Figure 3.3). Each retailer forms its own policy based on the policy resources. The set of retailer policies as a whole plus an enterprise-wide policy comprise the enterprise privacy policy which will be managed. Each of the retailer policies are determined based on the policy resources, one of which is the enterprise-wide policy.

In this section, we present a systematic approach to determining enterprise privacy policy from the set of policy resources.

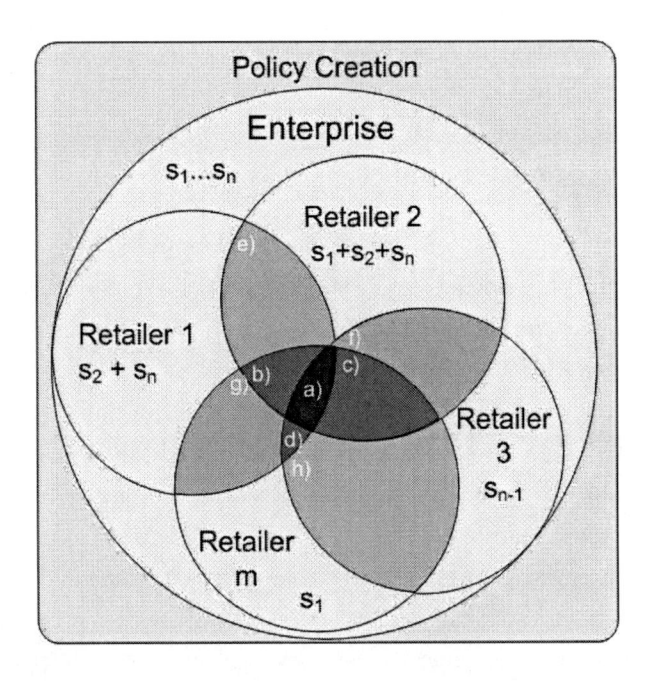

Figure 3.12: The enterprise, the enterprise subsets (called *retailers*), and the policy resources that influence each retailer.

3.2.3.1 Assumptions for privacy policy creation

We assume that the set of policy resources is not being represented in real-time. This is possible, but given the dynamic and interactive properties of the set of policy resources the approach is to consider the set at a snapshot in time.

We assume that if we can determine one retailer's privacy policy from two policy resources, our approach can be generalized for more than two policy resources. We also assume that the process used for one retailer is generalizable to the other retailers.

The properties described for managing enterprise privacy policy creation are assumed to apply to the retailers that comprise the enterprise.

We assume an enterprise with different policies for different retailers has an overall enterprise policy stating information collected under one retailer's policy must not be shared with retailers following a different policy.

The process related in this section is dependent on expressing the policy rules in a computer-readable format. The procedure for satisfying this dependency in this thesis is by manual analysis.

3.2.3.2 Systematic approach to policy creation

To combine the contributing sets into a managed enterprise privacy policy, E, we begin with our n policy resources contributing sets, $s_1, s_2, \cdots, s_n$, ordered from the highest weight ($weight(s_1)$) to the lowest weight ($weight(s_n)$) (where weight is as defined in Section 3.2.2.2). Consider the set $P = s_1 \cup s_2 \cup \cdots \cup s_n$, the set of all privacy policy rules in our set of policy resources. For each policy rule $p \in P$, we have a vector $(v = \{v_1, v_2, \cdots, v_n\})$, where n is the number of policy resources in our set. The values of this vector are determined according to Equation 3.1. If a policy rule exists in a given contributing set, the ith value (v_i) is the value of the 'weight' property of that policy resource; otherwise, the value is 0. The result is a vector v containing the weight each policy resource associates with a given policy rule (where the weight is 0 if the policy resource does not contain that policy rule).

$$v_i = \begin{cases} weight(s_i) & \text{if } p \in s_i \\ 0 & \text{otherwise} \end{cases} \quad (3.1)$$

We define the *overall weight* of a policy rule p using the L^1-norm of the vector v associated with p (Equation 3.2), where a policy rule's overall weight is a measure that combines the weights assigned by different policy resources to determine the relative importance of enforcing the policy rule.

$$weight(p) = ||v||_1 \quad (3.2)$$

The L^1-norm of v is equivalent to the sum of each of the n elements of v (Equation 3.3).

$$\sum_{k=1}^{n} v_k \quad (3.3)$$

A specific example of determining the weight of each individual policy rule is illustrated in Figure 3.13.

Once we have determined the weight for each of the policy rules in P, we set a threshold. A policy rule p exists in E, the set representing the enterprise privacy

$$s_1 = \{p_1,\ p_2,\ p_3\},\ weight = 20$$
$$s_2 = \{p_1,\ p_2,\ p_4\},\ weight = 5$$
$$s_3 = \{p_1,\ p_3,\ p_4\},\ weight = 1$$

$$p_1v = \{20,\ 5,\ 1\}$$
$$p_2v = \{20,\ 5,\ 0\}$$
$$p_3v = \{20,\ 0,\ 1\}$$
$$p_4v = \{\ 0,\ 5,\ 1\}$$

$$weight(p_1) = ||p_1v||_1 = 20 + 5 + 1 = 26$$
$$weight(p_2) = ||p_2v||_1 = 20 + 5 + 0 = 25$$
$$weight(p_3) = ||p_3v||_1 = 20 + 0 + 1 = 21$$
$$weight(p_4) = ||p_4v||_1 = 0 + 5 + 1 = 6$$

Figure 3.13: An example of determining the weights of individual privacy policy rules based on three sample policy resources, s_1, s_2, and s_3.

policy, if its weight (given by Equation 3.2) exceeds the minimum threshold. The weights and the threshold must be chosen to ensure that the policy rules from essential policy resources (e.g., legal and contractual obligations) are adopted.

We represent this selection process using a decision support matrix (M). Each column represents a policy resource ($s_1, \cdots, s_{n-1}, s_n$); each row represents a policy rule ($p \in P$). The value of the matrix in row i and column j is determined according to Equation 3.4.

$$M_{i,j} = \begin{cases} weight(s_j) & \text{if } p_i \in s_j \\ 0 & \text{otherwise} \end{cases} \quad (3.4)$$

The total weight of a policy rule p_i is equal to the sum of the elements in row i. We can also define additional measures; for example, an "Is this a legal requirement?" column based on the value of columns representing policy resources that can be legally enforced. An example using this method for the same values as Figure 3.13 is shown in Figure 3.14, where the "Legal Req." indicates whether or not p_i is required by legislation. In this example, if the threshold is set at 23, p_1 and p_2 will be chosen because they exceed the threshold; p_3 will also be chosen since it is a legal requirement. An example of the matrix method using concrete examples of policy rules and policy resources is shown in Figure 3.15.

$$s_1 = \{p_1, p_2, p_3\}, \ weight = 20$$
$$s_2 = \{p_1, p_2, p_4\}, \ weight = 5$$
$$s_3 = \{p_1, p_3, p_4\}, \ weight = 1$$

	s_1	s_2	s_3	$weight(p_i)$	Legal Req.
p_1	20	5	1	26	yes
p_2	20	5	0	25	yes
p_3	20	0	1	21	yes
p_4	0	5	1	6	no

Figure 3.14: Determining the weights of individual privacy policies using the matrix method.

Policy rules that exceed the threshold may conflict with one another. This will occur in the case where two or more heavily weighted policy resources have conflicting requirements (one example is a contract with terms that violate a newly passed piece of legislation). These policy conflicts should be detected automatically and resolved either automatically or manually. One solution is to resolve the conflicting requirements of the policy resources (for example, to renegotiate a contract). Another is to divide the enterprise into retailers in such a way that the two conflicting policy rules apply to two different retailers.

3.2.4 Resultant privacy policies

The result of policy creation is a privacy policy (q_i) for each of the m retailers ($r_1, r_2, r_i, \cdots, r_m$) that comprise the enterprise (Figure 3.16). There will be elements common to all of the retailers (Figure 3.12a; $q_1 \cap q_2 \cap \cdots \cap q_m$). There will also be an overall enterprise privacy policy (E) that governs the interactions among each of the retailers and among other organizations within the enterprise. These policies are

	International Law	National Law	Local Law	Consumer Requirements	Enterprise Policy	Contracts	Industry Standards	Legal Requirement?	Desirability Score
Provide written privacy policy to customers	1	1	1	1	1	1	1	Yes	14
Provide written privacy policy to customers - before any transaction begins	0	1	1	1	0	0	0	Yes	7
Provide written privacy policy to customers - in easy-to-understand language	0	0	0	1	1	0	0	No	4
Give individuals access to their own information	1	1	1	1	1	0	1	Yes	11
Give individuals access to their own information - free and with convenient online access	0	0	0	1	1	0	0	No	4
Do not share information with third parties under any circumstances	0	0	0	1	0	0	0	No	3
Share information with third parties only with customer consent	0	1	1	1	1	1	0	Yes	11

Figure 3.15: A concrete example of using the matrix method to determine the weights of individual privacy policies. In this case, the weights are added afterward when computing the overall weight ("desirability factor").

stored in a policy repository at each retailer that in addition to update and retrieval functions provides version control and policy conflict resolution. The enterprise has a central privacy policy repository that stores every retailer's policies and a set of "best practices" privacy policy templates for new retailers.

As an example, consider Wal-Mart as an enterprise consisting of a set of retailers. Wal-Mart is an international enterprise with stores in countries around the world. The executive officers of Wal-Mart would determine at what granularity to divide the enterprise into a set of retailers. One choice would be based on the state/province/locality of each country. For instance, two retailers in Canada would be Wal-Mart Quebec and Wal-Mart Nova Scotia. Each retailer would consist of all the stores in that state/province/locality. The policy resources for each retailer would include, for example, provincial and federal law and consumer perspectives. Some policy rules preferred by Quebec consumers would also be preferred by Nova Scotia consumers; however, there would be differences between the two. Wal-Mart Nova Scotia would be required to comply with federal privacy legislation; Wal-Mart Quebec would instead be required to comply with substantially similar provincial legislation. Additionally,

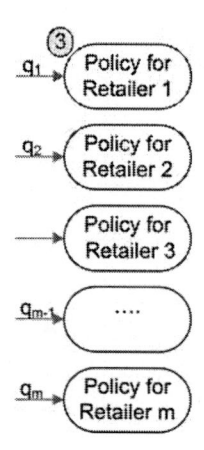

Figure 3.16: The privacy policies that result from policy creation.

Wal-Mart Quebec would be required to represent its policies in French. The resultant privacy policies for those two retailers would have overlap; a third retailer, Wal-Mart Texas, would have less overlap. There might be a certain core of privacy policy rules to which all or almost all retailers would be required to adhere.

Wal-Mart headquarters in Arkansas, United States would record the policies of each of its retailers, and from them could determine a set of policies that would apply to all retailers in addition to each retailer's own privacy policy. If a new Wal-Mart retailer were created (Wal-Mart Nunavut), its initial privacy policy could be based on stored policies from retailers with similar policy resources.

3.2.5 Validation, verification, deployment, and enforcement

Privacy policy *validation* addresses the question of whether or not the policy creation process is creating an enterprise privacy policy that meets the needs of the enterprise (and does the same for each of the retailers). It ensures that the policy contains critical elements that are required by the enterprise / retailer (see Figure 3.15). Privacy policy *verification* ensures that each of the elements of the created policy is consistent with the policy of the policy resource from which it was drawn. For example, consider a policy rule required by legislation stating "personal information must not be collected from children 13 years of age or younger". Privacy policy validation would ensure that this policy rule is in the enterprise privacy policy. Privacy policy verification would ensure that the policy rule as expressed in the enterprise privacy policy accurately reflects the requirements of the legislation.

Privacy policy *deployment* disseminates the created, verified, and validated privacy policies to the employees of each of the retailers and to any other enterprise employees to whom the policy is relevant. The employees may be trained in how to appropriately handle information according to the policy (Figure 3.17ii). The business processes of the enterprise and its retailers are examined to ensure each complies with the privacy policy (Figure 3.17i). Finally, the software used by the enterprise must be updated (This may be a design change, a configuration change, an implementation change, or all or none of the above for internally developed software, or a request for a vendor patch or a switch to an alternate software application for purchased software) (Figure 3.17iii).

Privacy policy *enforcement* ensures that the deployment phase has adequately implemented changes based on the policy. It is also a way to ensure the environment has not changed without corresponding changes in the privacy policy. *Employees* may receive refresher courses, random checks from the chief privacy officer, or privacy certification exams. Managers may be required to complete a report on their employees describing the implementation of the privacy policy. *Business processes* will undergo regular privacy impact assessments to determine the privacy risks to the process and to the overall enterprise. Software applications must be tested to ensure compliance with the privacy policy.

3.2.5.1 Testing software applications for privacy policy compliance

There is a need to test that new or existing software applications comply with an enterprise privacy policy. Privacy compliance testing provides a policy, configuration and implementation assessment process to mitigate risk and ensure compliance with privacy and security policies, government regulations, and industry standards. It also helps identify security and privacy issues related to critical business assets.

Software in need of privacy compliance testing may be acquired in one of four ways:

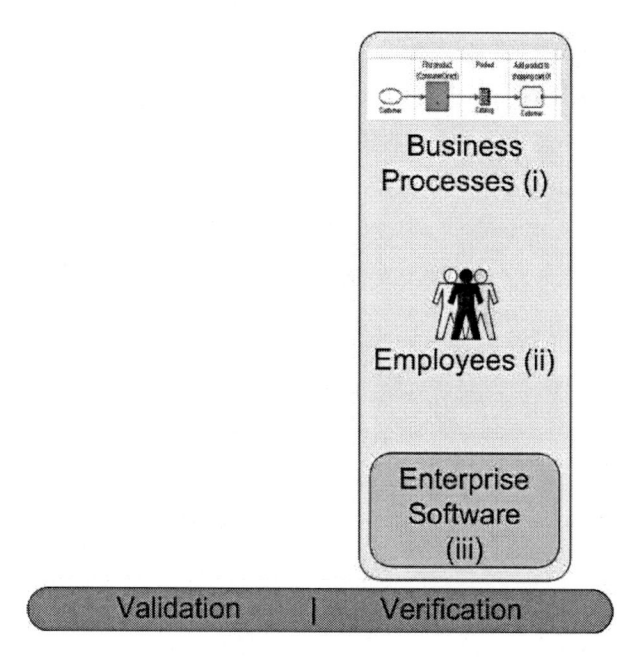

Figure 3.17: The policy must be validated with the original policy resources and deployed to business processes, employees, and software.

1. The application is developed in-house. The enterprise privacy policy will be considered during the requirement phases and implemented during the design phase of the software application, and privacy compliance testing will verify the implementation complies with the policy. For applications developed before the deployment of the privacy policy, appropriate privacy protections must be added to the software in an upgrade. Manual code inspection could work in this situation.

2. The application is modified from an existing open-source solution. Privacy protections must be retrofitted to the existing application, and the development team may not be as familiar with the source code. Manual code inspection could work in this situation.

3. The application is purchased "off the shelf" from a software vendor. The vendor may do some type of privacy compliance testing. To the enterprise, the software

application is a 'black box', and code inspection will not work.

4. The application is custom-built by a software vendor, or is purchased from a software vendor and customized in-house. The custom building process may include privacy compliance testing, as might the customization. Some portions of the software application might be available for code inspection, while the remainder will be a 'black box'.

Our approach considers the software application to be a black box, with one exception: the application can be divided into sub-components that mark different access and exit points for information input and output. This approach works for each of the means enumerated above. However, it does not completely replace other approaches to software testing. When testing by code inspection, for example, testers should be familiar with privacy policies and common breaches of privacy policies.

An enterprise privacy policy governs the configuration of, manipulation of, and access to personal information by the enterprise. As it applies to software, it governs the processing of personal information by that software application. Testing software for compliance with the policy involves tracing the movement of information through the software application and to or from outside entities, followed by a determination of whether or not this information is personal and if so the degree of sensitivity.

The movement of information through a software application is dictated by a set of *workflows*. A workflow is "the operational aspect of a work procedure: how tasks are structured, who performs them, what their relative order is, how they are synchronized, how information flows to support the tasks, and how tasks are being tracked" [129]. A shopping workflow and the order product sub-workflow (describing the process of finding a product to order), as described by IBM's WebSphere Commerce software application, is shown in Figure 2.5. The workflow for placing an order (or "checking out") is shown in Figure 3.18. The customer can either do a quick checkout or a regular checkout. If the customer chooses regular checkout, they will be prompted for their billing address, shipping address, and preferred shipment method. If quick checkout is chosen, this information will be loaded from a stored profile (if one does not exist, the customer is asked to create one). In either case, an order summary will be displayed to confirm the information is correct, the customer will

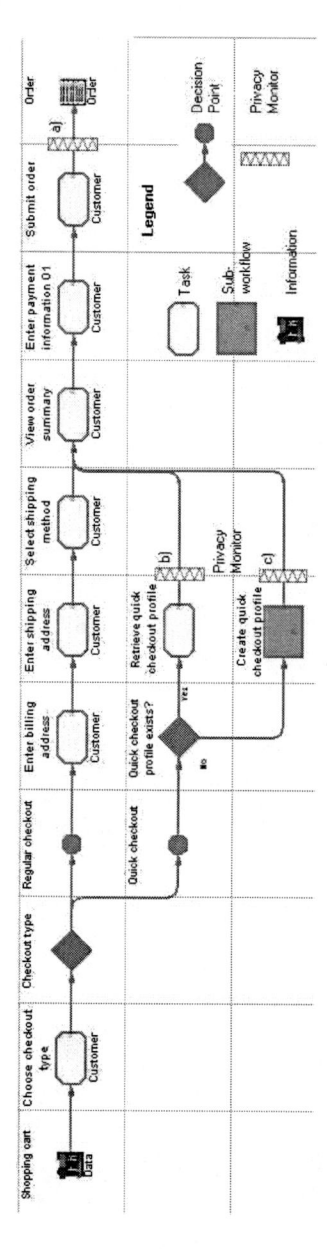

Figure 3.18: Workflow for creating an order on an e-commerce website (modified from [67]), showing the privacy monitor filters.

be asked to enter payment information, and finally will submit the order. The order is then stored in the retailer's database.

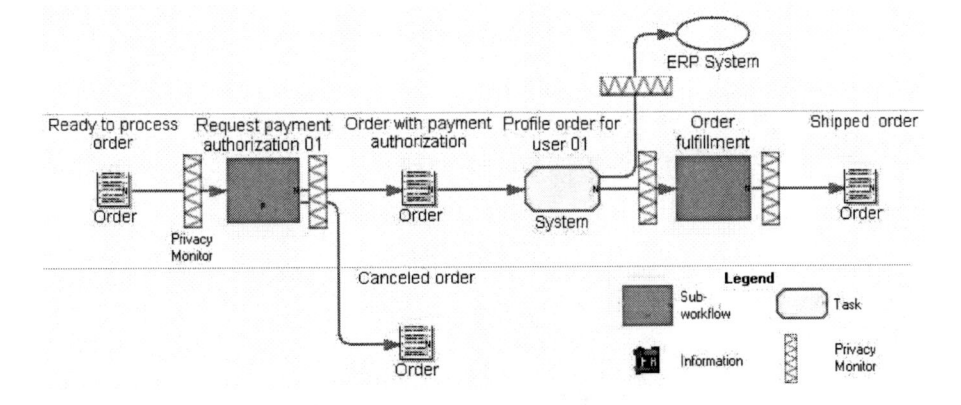

Figure 3.19: Workflow for processing an e-commerce order (modified from [68]) showing the privacy monitor filters.

A subsequent workflow for processing an order once places is shown in Figure 3.19. Using the information stored in the order created by the workflow shown in Figure 3.18, the payment details will be authorized with the appropriate financial institution. The result will be either a canceled or an authorized order, which is stored in the customer's profile for use in recommending future purchases. The order is also recorded in an Enterprise Resource Planning (ERP) System that manages the retailer's resources. The approved order is passed to a fulfillment subprocess which packages the order, updates the inventory, transmits the delivery information to the delivery agent, and notifies the customer.

These workflows are enabled by the flow of information from one task to the next. We call each movement of information an *information flow*. An information flow is a set of data elements that are sent from one entity to another or from one task to another (A *data element* is a single data value and an associated data descriptor; an *entity* is any discrete unit like an individual, business unit, organization, or a corporation). Each of the arrows in the workflow diagrams shown in Figure 3.18 and Figure 3.19 indicates that information (or control of the information) is passing from one task to another or from one entity to another. This research focuses on

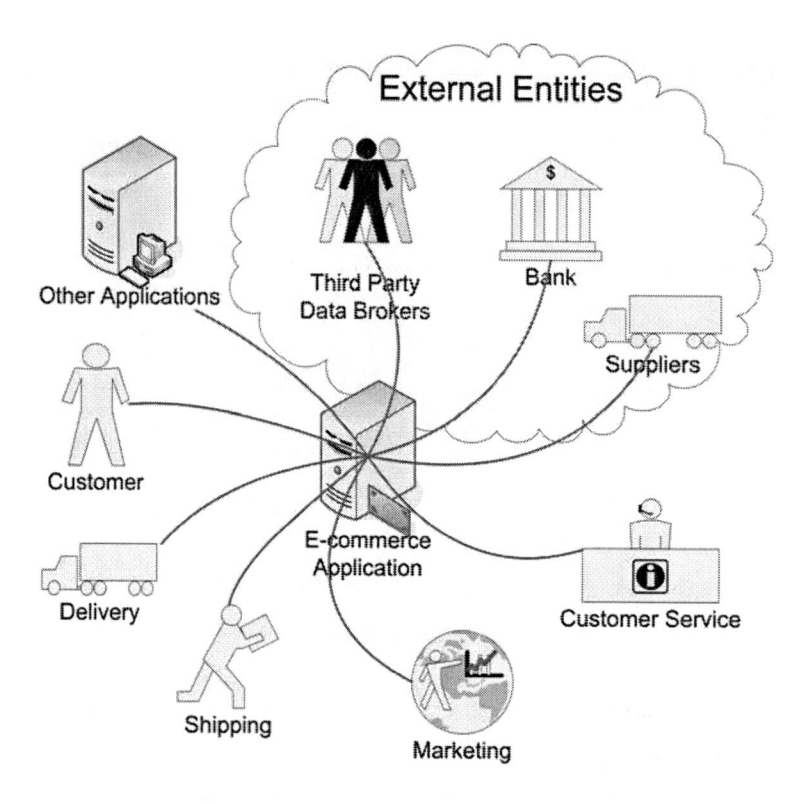

Figure 3.20: Example information handlers in e-commerce.

information flows that involve the application (e.g., where one of the two entities is the application, or where information passes through the application when transmitted from one entity to the next).

Figure 3.18 shows privacy monitors (later implemented as Filters in Java) at various points throughout the workflow (a,b,c). Privacy monitor a examines the flow of information to create the order as submitted by the customer and ensures it complies with the retailer's privacy policies. Privacy monitor b examines the personal information contained in the quick checkout profile retrieved by the system from the database. Privacy monitor c examines the personal information submitted by the customer in the sub-workflow that creates a quick checkout profile. Figure 3.19 also shows privacy monitors. They check the information being sent to a financial institution, the information retrieved from the financial institution, the information being saved to the ERP system, the information before it is sent to shipping and delivery, and the information received from the delivery agent.

When examining the information, the privacy monitor compares the transmission of the information (including the destination, source, and the presence of personal information) to the enterprise privacy policies. If a violation is detected, the privacy monitor may take one or more actions including halting the transaction, warning the customer, asking for additional consent, or notifying the administrator. Privacy compliance is tested at multiple points in the workflow to achieve the minimum possible exposure of personal information; namely, after information is collected from the customer, before information is stored in persistent storage, after information is stored in persistent storage, before information is sent to an external entity, and after information is retrieved from an external entity. These privacy monitors are part of a privacy compliance testing methodology. Our implementation will focus on privacy monitor a and c in Figure 3.18, which monitor information submitted by the customer. This privacy monitor can be implemented during the deployment or testing phases of software applications, during the production phase of software applications, or both.

We call the entities that send or receive information *sources* and *destinations* of information, depending on their role. A single entity may be both a source and destination. Figure 3.20 shows some of the sources and destinations in electronic commerce. A module of the e-commerce application receives that request and can serve as a manager or dispatcher of the sources and destinations, and the determiner of which destination receives information from which sources, and when. Information may be transmitted to other applications (e.g., a user authentication server or a data-mining product) or to external entities like third party data brokers or the enterprise's suppliers. Internally, customer service personnel, shipping personnel or sales/marketing personnel might access the information. The delivery agent may be an external entity. The customer submits an order via a website and interacts with the application.

The information flows can be grouped by the specific communication medium through which they pass, as shown in Figure 3.21. Information flows to external entities are transmitted via the Internet. Flows to other applications are transmitted

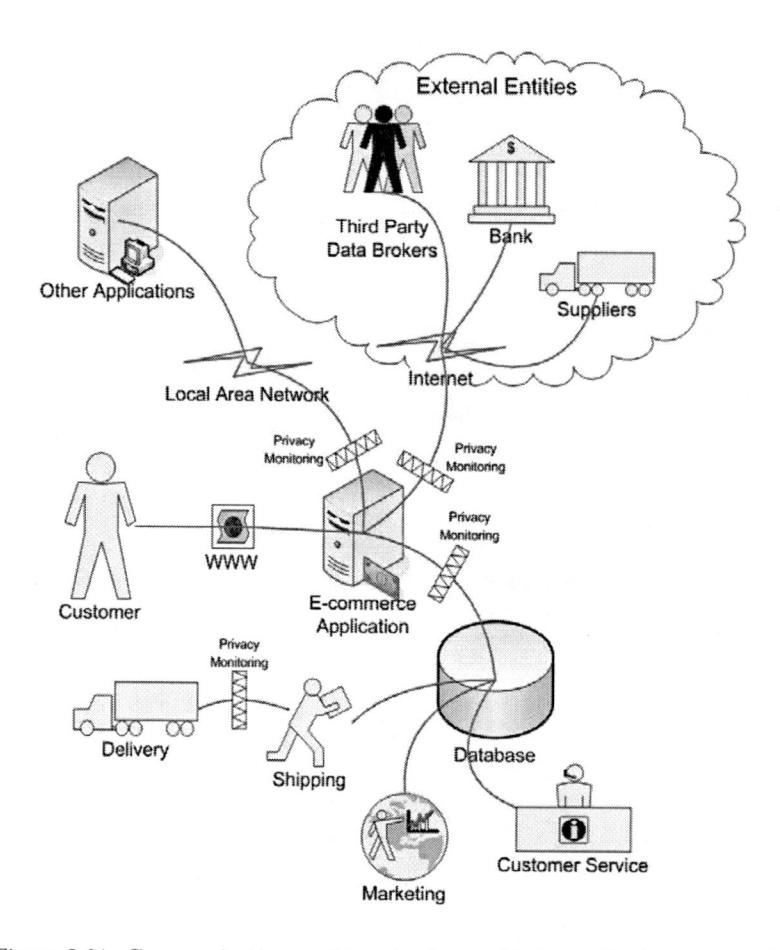

Figure 3.21: Communication medium for flows of information in an example e-commerce transaction.

via the local area network. The e-commerce server stores information to a database, where it is accessed by internal business units and as needed by the e-commerce server. The customer communicates with the e-commerce server through the world wide web on the Internet.

3.2.5.2 Privacy compliance testing methodology

The second part of our methodology is to provide a privacy compliance testing, as follows:

1. **Rule Generation.** From the enterprise privacy policy, generate a set of rules determining permissible information flows. The format of these rules can be determined by the information available to the tester in the Rule Evaluation step (4).

2. **Capture Information Flows.** For each of the communication mediums employed by the software application (e.g., Figure 3.21), capture information as it is transmitted to and from the software application from and to other entities. The source and destination of the information should be captured; if the application is the source or destination, the module of the application responsible for sending or receiving the information should be recorded.

3. **Understand Information Flows.** The data elements in the captured information flows consist of a data value and a data descriptor. The descriptor is assigned by the application and is a specific name. We "understand" its meaning by mapping it to a pre-defined label that is understood. For example, the application-specific data descriptors 'user_name', 'firstName', '$u' would map to the pre-defined label 'name'. The abstracted label has a meaning, it is known to be personal information, and it has a level of sensitivity as determined by the enterprise privacy policy. Its meaning can also be understood by 'grouping' the data descriptor with other descriptors. For example, 'age' and 'gender' might be grouped and assigned the label of 'demographics'. Grouped descriptors have properties similar to and levels of sensitivity identical to those of other descriptors in the same group and can be treated the same way. Non-personal information not relevant to the privacy compliance testing can be added to a single group and subsequently ignored.

4. **Rule Evaluation.** The rules established in step 1 are applied to the information flows. Flows of information that do not comply with the rules are identified. Given the policy rule in the enterprise privacy policy responsible for the violated

rule, we can determine the weight calculated in the creation step and assign a weight to this violation.

5. **Report on Compliance.** The outcome of the rules-based analysis in the Rule Evaluation step (4) is reported. Different formats may be required for different consumers. Programmers assigned to resolve compliance errors will require more detail than a manager required to review testing progress. The output can include which module of the software may be non-compliant and why, which data elements were transmitted by non-compliant information flows, the rule that was violated, how the rule was violated, and the original source of the rule.

3.3 Summary

A framework for privacy policy management was proposed, based on our requirements, assumptions and defined properties. This framework shows how the components of enterprise privacy policy management software interact to create, deploy, and enforce enterprise privacy policy.

A methodology for managing enterprise privacy policy is summarized in Figure 3.22. The figure shows the enterprise as a collection of retailers. The enterprise is obliged to comply with a set of privacy requirements (e.g. laws) and has incentive to meet an additional set of privacy expectations (e.g. meeting consumer privacy expectations) which can result in improved relationships with certain stakeholders (e.g., consumers). Each retailer contained in the enterprise is affected by a variable combination of these influences, called policy resources $(s_1, s_2, \cdots, s_n)$. For example, Retailer 1 is affected by s_2 (privacy laws) and s_n (the enterprise itself). Each enterprise may be affected by a different set of policy resources. Each retailer forms its own policy based on its policy resources. These policies collectively comprise the enterprise privacy policy.

A retailer's policies will have elements in common with other retailers with similar policy resources, similar sectors of industry, similar target markets, and similar applicable legislation. The enterprise will have elements in common with other enterprises for the same reasons. The *core elements* of an enterprise's privacy policy are pictured in Figure 3.22(2)a (the intersection of each of the sets), and will be present in each

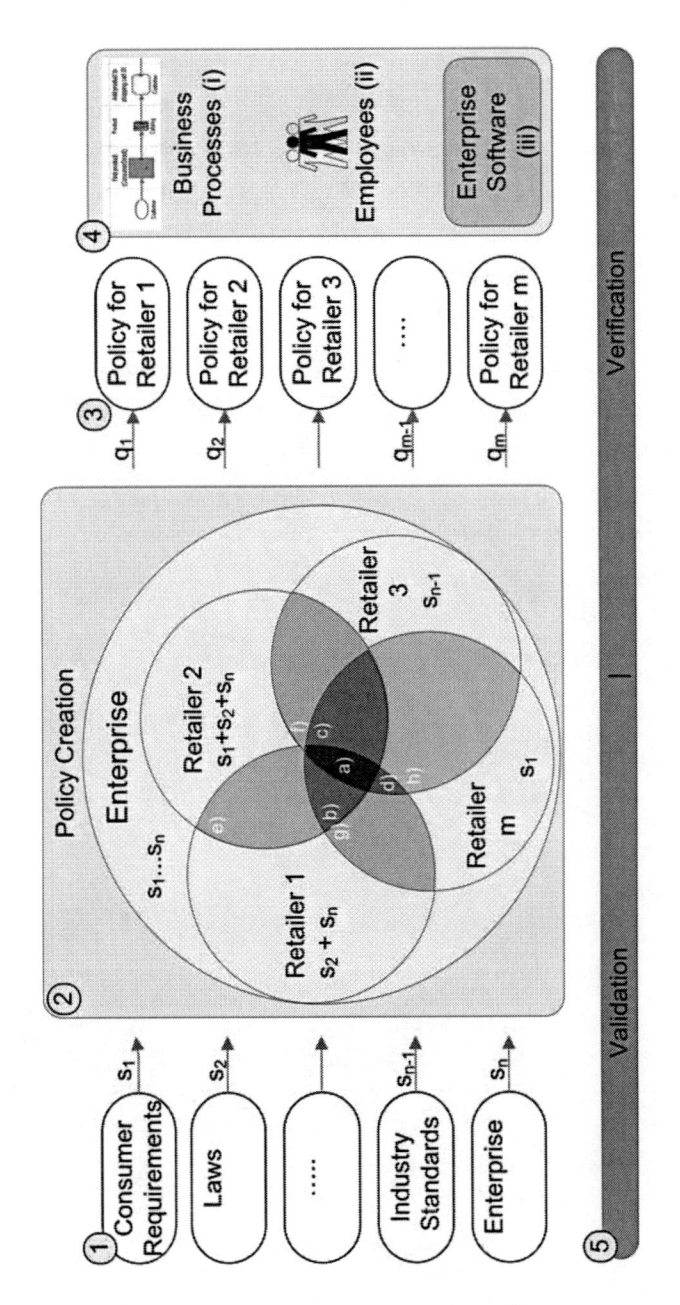

Figure 3.22: Overall view of enterprise privacy policy management.

of the retailer's privacy policies.

As these policies are defined they will be disseminated within the organization. Employees, processes, and software must comply with the policy (deployment). The policy and compliance with the policy will be validated and verified. The policy will be enforced on non-compliant employees, processes, and software. The results of the dissemination/deployment/compliance/enforcement steps will influence subsequent versions of the enterprise privacy policy.

Finally, a second methodology, for testing software for compliance with a privacy policy, was described. E-commerce workflows are modified to include monitoring the flows of information for compliance with a set of privacy rules extracted from the enterprise privacy policy. Flows of information are captured, abstracted to well-understood data types, compared to privacy rules, and reported on.

Chapter 4

Implementation and Results

In this chapter, we test our hypotheses by implementing two modules of the framework described in Chapter 3. Our proof-of-concept creation of enterprise privacy policy based on two policy resources is based on the framework and methodology in Section 3.2 and is discussed in Section 4.1. Our proof-of-concept implementation of the automated privacy compliance testing methodology proposed in Section 3.2.5 is discussed in Section 4.2; the results of this implementation are in Section 4.3. The two modules we implement are shown as part of the enterprise privacy management framework in Figure 4.1.

4.1 Enterprise Privacy Policy Creation

A sample enterprise privacy policy was created by determining the policy privacy requirements of two policy resources: legislation (Canada's *PIPED Act* [7]) and the enterprise's promise to its consumers (posted P3P and plain-text privacy policies). We determine and represent the two policy resources using the framework described in Section 3.2.

The legislation policy resource was described as one of the most important policy resources in Section 3.2.2.4, and therefore was chosen as one of the policy resources we consider. The retailer's promise to its consumers by way of a P3P policy was chosen as a sample policy resource because breaking a promise to a consumer is illegal, regardless of whether or not the promise is privacy-related. Additional policy resources were not examined, but we expect that fundamentally the analysis would proceed similarly to the two we selected. The first policy resource to be included is consumer preferences, which are a powerful influence on enterprise privacy policy.

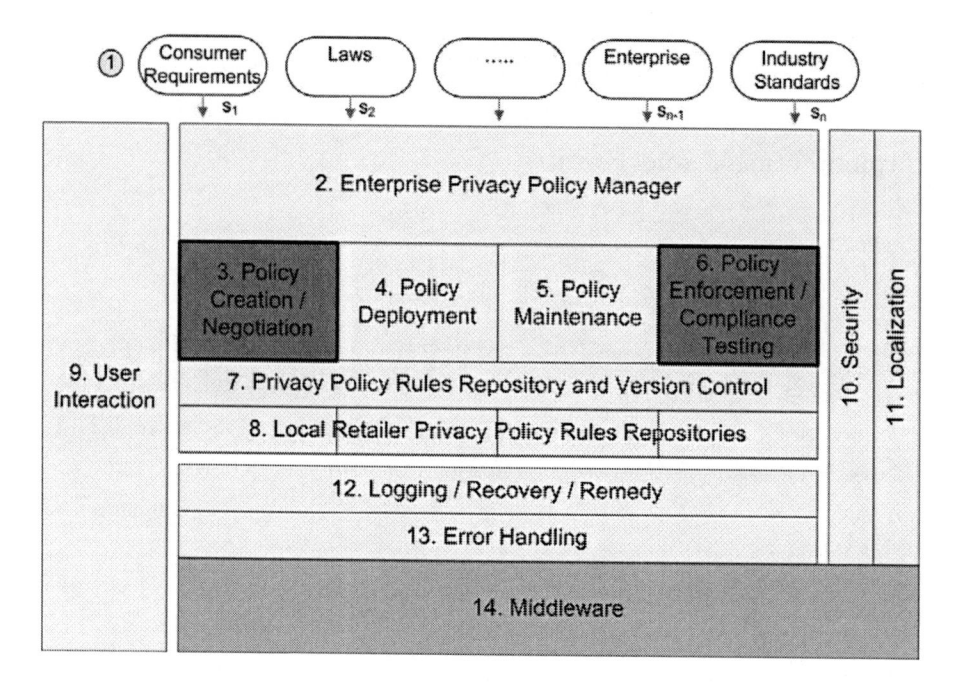

Figure 4.1: The two modules of the enterprise privacy policy management software framework implemented in this chapter (3 and 6).

4.1.1 Privacy legislation

To determine the requirements of the Legislation policy resource, legislation was manually analyzed. For this proof-of-concept implementation, we primarily used one article of legislation (the PIPEDA [7]). This is the law applicable to all private enterprise in Canada; in Section 2.1.2, we showed that its principles were similar to the principles of privacy legislation in Europe. To demonstrate that our framework was capable of representing more than one article of legislation, we included several requirements from other pieces of legislation, including one from another jurisdiction.

The *Personal Information Protection and Electronic Documents Act* addresses "Personal Information Protection" in Part 1 and Schedule 1. Schedule 1 lists the principles of privacy that the Act enforces as law, which we summarize in Section 2.1.2. The requirements extracted in this proof-of-concept analysis are from principles 1, 3, and 7. Table 4.1 shows the complete list of proof-of-concept legislative requirements.

Source	Impact	Requirement text
PIPEDA 4.1.3	warning	Information may be transferred to a third party only if that third party is bound to handle the information in the same way as the enterprise
PIPEDA 4.3.7	warning	When completing an online form containing personal information, there must be a consent checkbox
PIPEDA 4.7.2	error	Sensitive information must be encrypted during transmission
PIPEDA 4.7.2	error	Information in the cookies or the URL must be encrypted during transmission
Multiple [9]	error	The Social Insurance Number or Social Security Number must not be collected
COPPA [6]	error	Personal information must not be collected from individuals under the age of 13

Table 4.1: Requirements manually derived from legislation, with the severity of violations (warning or error).

An attempt was made to use part-of-speech tagging and look for noun and action verb sequences in Schedule 5 of *PIPEDA* [7] to reduce the amount of manual work required to create computer-readable policies, or potentially to automate the process completely. Synonym sets were used to reduce and standardize the possible vocabulary. The most common phrases and common sequences of nouns and action verbs were extracted, and human inspection converted these to enforceable rules. The most common action verbs are listed in Table 4.2. This approach did not work noticeably faster than the time required for a human to inspect the entire legislative document. Further, the vague wording of the legislation [79] indicates that important portions of the legislation would be missed by this method. Although this approach to requirement determination may be viable, more research and implementation would be required to determine its feasibility for this type of analysis. Therefore, this implementation was discarded in favour of a domain-expert reviewing the law and generating several rules.

4.1.2 Existing enterprise privacy policy

Online retailers may post their privacy policies online using the Platform for Privacy Preferences (P3P) (see Section 2.3.1.1). The requirements of this policy resource are

Verb	Occurrences
disclose	31
include	18
provide	16
give	15
apply	14
collect	10
identified	10
send	9
comply	8
respond	8

Table 4.2: Most common action verbs in *PIPEDA*.

determined by automatically examining a P3P file downloaded from an online retailer (in our case, IBM's P3P policy [62]). We then applied a set of criteria to certain P3P elements to determine a translation from P3P into a set of enforceable rules. The P3P elements examined are listed in Table 4.3; for this implementation, the P3P elements were limited to what personal information could be collected, and to which organizations information could be sent.

Element	Sub-Element(s)	Rule text
<NON-IDENTIFIABLE>	–	No personal information may be collected.
<RECIPIENT>	Only <delivery/>	Information may be sent to any entity other than a delivery agent.
<RECIPIENT>	Only <ours/>	Information may not be sent to any third parties.
<RECIPIENT>	<unrelated/>	This is a policy conflict with the legislation policy resource.
<DATA-GROUP>	<DATA>	Any data elements that are part of the P3P data schema and not listed here may not be collected from the user.

Table 4.3: Criteria for deriving requirements from P3P policies.

4.2 Testing Software Applications for Privacy Compliance

The privacy compliance testing methodology described in Section 3.2.5.2 was implemented using IBM WebSphere Commerce (Section 2.2.5) as the e-commerce software application. The implementation is general and designed to work for any J2EE-compliant application, especially retailer stores developed on WebSphere Commerce, but was tested specifically using the ConsumerDirect B2C store model that is distributed with WebSphere Commerce. This proof-of-concept implementation follows a component-based architecture, where the functionality specified in each step of the privacy compliance testing methodology is provided by a single component. The five main components are the *capture component* (a), the *abstraction component* (b), the *analysis component* (d), and the *display component* (e). A specification for a *context component* (c) is included but not implemented or discussed (the context component is included to account for the possibility that contextual information about the use and manipulation of the information inside the application is relevant to testing privacy policy compliance). These components are illustrated in Figure 4.2; detailed discussion of the first four components may be found in Sections 4.2.2 through 4.2.5. A broad overview of the components is given in Section 3.2.5.2, where steps 2, 3, 4 and 5 correspond to the capture, abstraction, analysis, and display components, respectively. The entire implementation is part of a Java package, `org.dalhousie.pct` (Figure 4.4).

Each component adheres to a specified interface (named *X*Component), and a minimal implementation (named Base*X*Component) is provided for each component interface. The implementation includes this set of interfaces and placeholder classes to define the architecture of the software application. These placeholder classes and other utility classes are pictured in a UML diagram[1], Figure 4.3. Any program or component complying with an interface may be used in place of the default implementation of that interface. All of the components implement an overall interface called Component (Figure 4.4a, shown also in Figure 4.3). The components communicate using the Information Flow Markup Language (IFML) (Section 4.2.1), and locate the next component necessary for processing using factory objects (Figure 4.4). In particular, the capture component uses the AbstractionComponentFactory (Figure 4.4b)

---

[1]The Unified Modeling Language (UML) is a specification that helps specify, visualize, and document models of software systems, including their structure and design [86]. A dependency diagram illustrates the dependencies between modules of the software application. The arrows point from a module to the module(s) on which it depends.

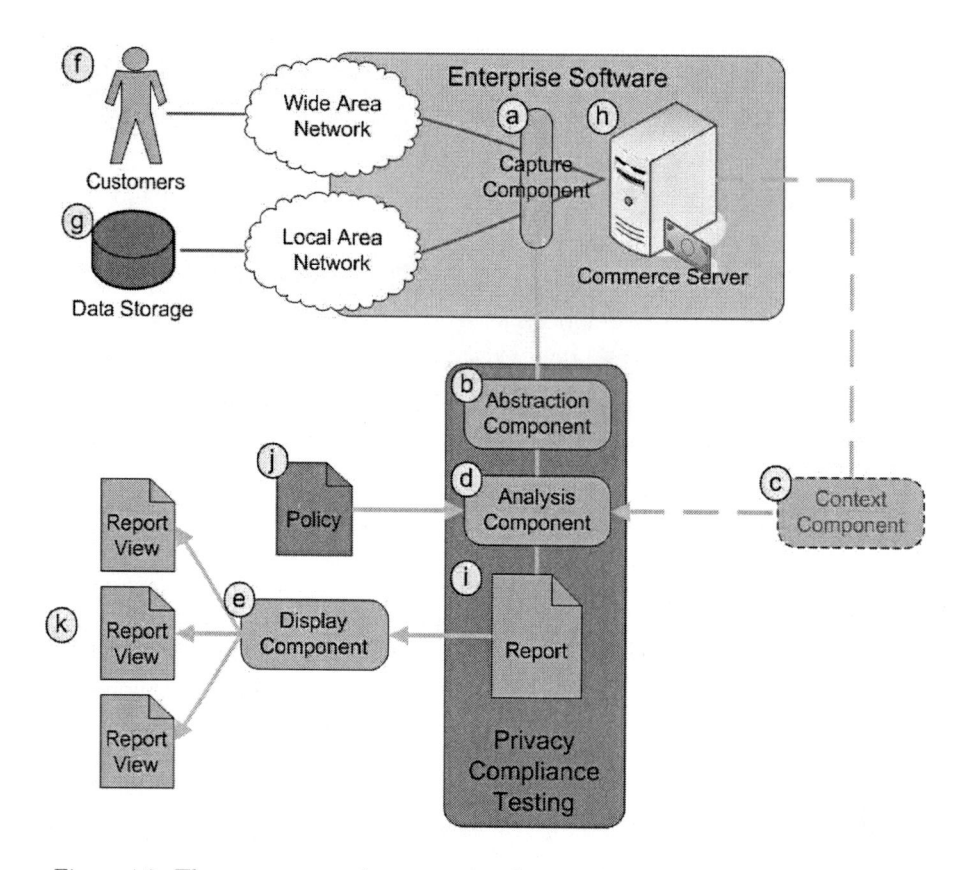

Figure 4.2: The components that comprise the proof-of-concept implementation of the privacy compliance testing for software applications.

to locate the abstraction component. The abstraction component uses the AnalysisComponentFactory (Figure 4.4d) to locate the analysis component. Finally, the analysis component may use the ContextComponentFactory (Figure 4.4c) to locate a context component.

4.2.1 Information flow markup language (IFML)

The privacy compliance testing components are distinct from one another and communicate by transmitting an XML document (or by providing a URL to an XML

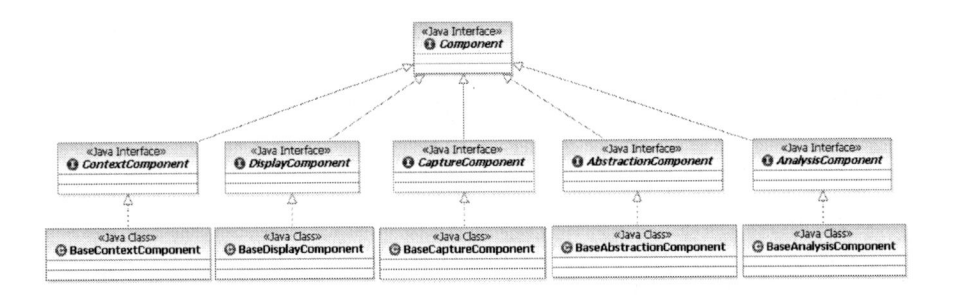

Figure 4.3: The interface hierarchy with the base implementation class that full implementations can extend (UML dependency diagram).

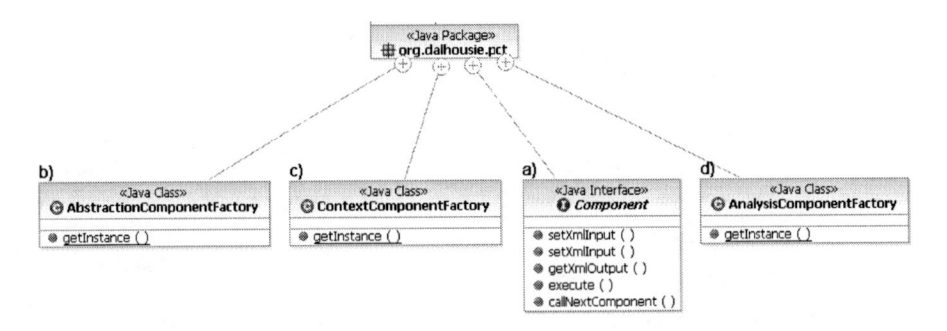

Figure 4.4: The factory objects that locate and return components.

document or the file location of an XML document). The XML document is formatted as specified by an XML-based language created both to allow communication and to allow representation / storage of a privacy compliance report. This language is called the the Information Flow Markup Language (IFML) (or more properly, the Privacy Compliance Testing Information Flow Markup Language (PCTIFML)). Information flows are the implementation of workflows, as described in Section 3.2.5.1.

The IFML document is incrementally developed as each component adds its own content. Once each component of the privacy compliance testing software has executed, the results of its execution are expressed using IFML. The final display component converts the IFML into a human-readable form; by this point, the IFML document contains information about the information flows and the rules with which the information flows do not comply. The outline of a standard IFML document is shown in Figure 4.5. IFML is defined using the XML Schema Definition (Appendix A).

```
<ifml>
  <application_subset name='LoginPage'>
     <source name="user">
        <data descriptor='user_name' label='name'
            sensitivity='1' secure='1'>value</data>
        <!-- more data elements -->
     </source>
     <destination name="user">
        <data descriptor='user_name' label='name'
            sensitivity='1' secure='1'>value</data>
        <!-- more data elements -->
     </destination>
     <!-- more sources and destinations -->
     <rule name="name of rule" message="explanation of rule"
            result="pass, fail, warn, or unknown" />
     <!-- more rules -->
  </application_subset>
  <!-- more application subsets-->
</ifml>
```

Figure 4.5: The XML outline of an IFML document.

An IFML document is organized into sections, each of which applies to a predefined subset of the software application being tested. These sections are defined by the `<application_subset>` element. Each `<application_subset>` element contains elements representing the information it sends and receives, organized by source and destination respectively. Thus, each `<application_subset>` element consists of a set of `<source>` and `<destination>` elements. Each of the `<source>` and `<destination>` elements contains a set of `<data>` elements. After execution of the analysis component (Figure 4.2d), each `<application_subset>` element is augmented with a set of `<rule>` elements that store the outcome of the rule-based analysis of compliance with a set of privacy requirements.

The `<application_subset>`, `<source>`, and `<destination>` elements have one attribute, the name of the application subset, source, or destination, respectively. Each of the the `<data>` elements has five attributes: the data descriptor, the abstracted data label, the sensitivity level, whether the element was transmitted securely, and a special attribute to store miscellaneous properties that are only relevant to certain types of data (e.g., the expiry date of the cookie in the case where the data element is stored in a cookie). The `<rule>` element has three attributes: the name of the rule, the plain English description of the rule, and whether that application subset passed or failed or generated a warning or warned that some data elements were unknown for the given rule.

A set of helper objects provides the core components with the functionality to write properly formatted IFML documents. Figure 4.6 shows the UML class diagram for IFMLHelper. The capture component calls the IFML helper object with the name of the application subset, the data element and its properties, and the source or destination of the data transfer. The IFML helper object generates the IFML document with duplicates removed, creating any `<application_subset>`, `<source>`, or `<destination>` elements as needed to add the `<data>` element. The abstraction component uses the IFML helper object to add abstracted data labels to the `<data>` elements. The analysis component calls the IFML helper object with the values of the `<rule>` attributes and the helper object adds the `<rule>` element to the appropriate `<application_subset>` element.

4.2.2 Capture component: capture information flows

The Capture Component (Figure 4.2a) captures information as it is transmitted to and from the software application (commerce server) (Figure 4.2h) from and to other

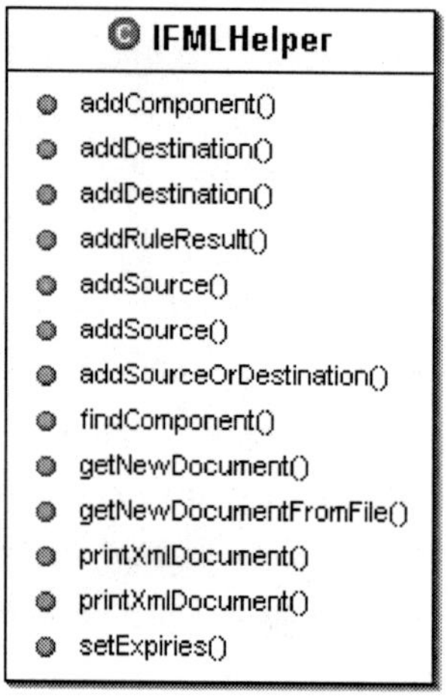

```
┌─────────────────────────────┐
│      ◉ IFMLHelper           │
├─────────────────────────────┤
│ ● addComponent()            │
│ ● addDestination()          │
│ ● addDestination()          │
│ ● addRuleResult()           │
│ ● addSource()               │
│ ● addSource()               │
│ ● addSourceOrDestination()  │
│ ● findComponent()           │
│ ● getNewDocument()          │
│ ● getNewDocumentFromFile()  │
│ ● printXmlDocument()        │
│ ● printXmlDocument()        │
│ ● setExpiries()             │
└─────────────────────────────┘
```

Figure 4.6: UML class diagram for the IFML Helper class.

entities. The output of the capture component is a list of transmissions to the application and from the application (the two-way interactions are converted into two one-way interactions). A given data element will be sent to the application by x entities and is said to have x sources. A given data element will be sent by the application to y entities, and is said to have y destinations. At least one of either x or y should be greater than zero.

The information flow is attained by determining, for each combination of source and destination entities, which data elements are sent from that source to that destination. The result of the capture is a tuple, $f = \{s, d, E\}$, where s is the source, d is the destination, and E is the information transmitted from s to d in the form of a set of tuples $\{v, n\}$ where v is a data value and n is the corresponding descriptor.

Multiple capture components may be required to capture information flows to and from multiple entities. The proof-of-concept implementation includes a capture component (Figure 4.2a) capable of capturing all information that is transmitted between the users (the customers, Figure 4.2f) and the software application (the commerce server, Figure 4.2h).

To capture the information transmitted to and by a Java Enterprise Edition (J2EE) application, such as IBM WebSphere Commerce (Section 2.2.5), we must

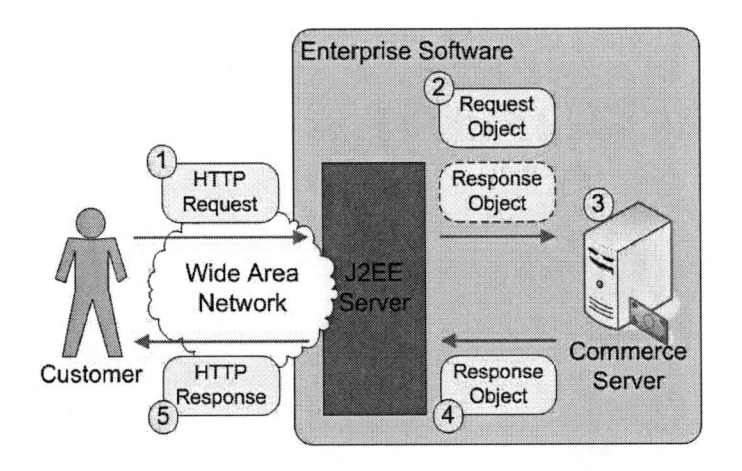

Figure 4.7: A basic customer interaction with a J2EE application.

understand a simplified customer interaction with a J2EE application (Figure 4.7).

1. The customer requests content from the web site. This request might include information submitted using a form and cookie information. The request is formulated by the customer's web browser (the *client*) and transmitted via HTTP or secure HTTP (HTTPS).

2. The J2EE server receives the request and encapsulates it in a *request object*. This object is passed to the web application running on the server, along with an empty response object. The subset of the application that receives the request and response objects is determined from the URL in the request.

3. The application receives the request and executes program logic on the commerce server. It determines what result (also called a response or a view) to return to the customer and fills the response object with the response.

4. The application returns a response object to the J2EE server.

5. The J2EE server extracts the response from the response object and transmits the response to the customer.

We capture the customer's request and the application's response by means of a

J2EE filter interposed between the customer and the application. The filter substitutes its own wrapper around the response object to overcome a J2EE limitation and track the response updates for later analysis (Figure 4.8).

The J2EE specification defines *filters* [111] that allow for pre-processing of request objects sent to and sent by the web application. A filter may be added to a web application without modifying the source code of the application and in such a way that it is transparent to the customers. The filter receives the same request object that the application would receive, and may both view and modify the request contents before the request object is passed to the target application (between steps 2 and 3 described above). Filters apply the same program logic to all requests, making them useful for authentication, logging, conversion from one encoding or format to another, and/or data compression. The filters used in this implementation are based on the Sun Intercepting Filter pattern [111] with custom extensions to allow modification of the response object.

The capture component (Figure 4.8) is implemented as a standard J2EE filter that captures the information contained in the client's request (Figure 4.9b). At the time the filter code is executed, the web application is not aware of the request and therefore has not generated a response. The filter sees the request object and an empty response object to which the web application will write output to the client. The information in the request object is accessed using the access methods. The J2EE specification does not provide any methods to read the contents of a response object; therefore, the filter must (1) be modified and (2) continue execution after the application has generated a response.

To capture the information written to the response object, a new object is created that contains the response object and mimics its behavior while introducing additional functionality to track the reads, writes, and updates of the response object. This new object is called a "wrapper" (see the ResponseCapture object, Figure 4.9f). This wrapper poses as the original response object and is sent to the application (Step 2.5 in Figure 4.8). The application writes to the ResponseCapture object as if it were the original response object. The ResponseCapture object stores all writes in a data structure before writing them to the original response object it contains. The basic customer interaction is altered in such a way that the ResponseCapture

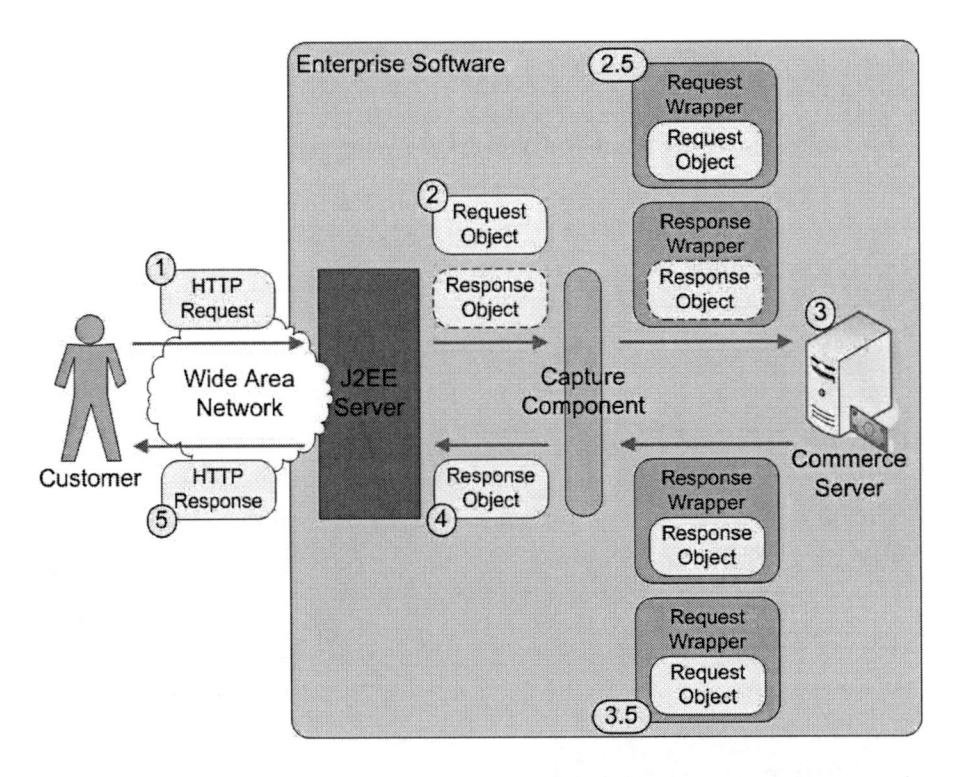

Figure 4.8: A customer's interaction with a J2EE application as modified to capture the customer's request and the application response.

object is returned to the filter rather than to the client (Step 3.5 in Figure 4.8). The information captured by the ResponseCapture object is saved to the IFML file by the capture component and the original response object is extracted and returned to the client (Step 4 in Figure 4.8). The request object passed on to the web application is similarly "wrapped" (Step 2.5 in Figure 4.8). The wrapper object (a RequestCapture object, Figure 4.9e) records the manipulations and accesses of the original request object and saves them to the IFML file.

On receipt of the wrapped request object, our filter (the capture component) first examines the request object. The data elements (tuples $\{v, n\}$, each consisting of a data descriptor n and a data value v submitted by the customer) are extracted from the request object. Parameters submitted with the HTTP request, parameters in the URL, and parameters retrieved from cookies are included in the request object in the form of name-value pairs. The name is stored as the data descriptor (n), and the value is stored as the data value (v).

The capture component next examines the response object. The response object consists of an HTML page, cookies to be created or updated, and a URL with parameters. We extract data elements from the cookie and URL based on the name-value pairs. We extract data elements from the HTML page by examining the template used to generate the HTML page. The template consists of static content and instructions to insert dynamic values. The dynamic values are the data elements we wish to capture, and will again be name-value pairs (the value is the value in the HTML page; the name is the variable name in the template). The JspDataParser (Figure 4.9d) is responsible for locating the JSP template and comparing the HTML page to the JSP template. (In IBM WebSphere Commerce, the location of the template (a Java Servlet Page, or JSP) is determined from an XML configuration file.)

For the requests, the source is the string "customer" or "user" and the destination is the string "software application". The subset of the application receiving the information is determined from the URL requested. For the responses, the source is the application and the destination is the customer. The subset of the application sending the information is determined from the URL returned by the response object. The application subsets in this implementation are divided based on the IBM WebSphere Commerce commands, where each command comprises a single application subset. For other implementations, the division would follow natural divisions where information flows to or from that application subset are detectable based on only information in the HTTP request or response.

Each captured data element and the source and destination is passed to the IFML generator class that adds it to an IFML document (see Section 4.2.1). The result is a document describing the information flows using tuples of the form $f = \{s, d, E\}$, where E is a set of data elements with a common source s and destination d.

To allow for the subsequent analysis, all captured information flows to or from the customer where the information is retrieved from or written to a URL or a cookie are additionally stored in the IFML file as flows to or from an entity called 'URL' and an entity named 'Cookie', respectively.

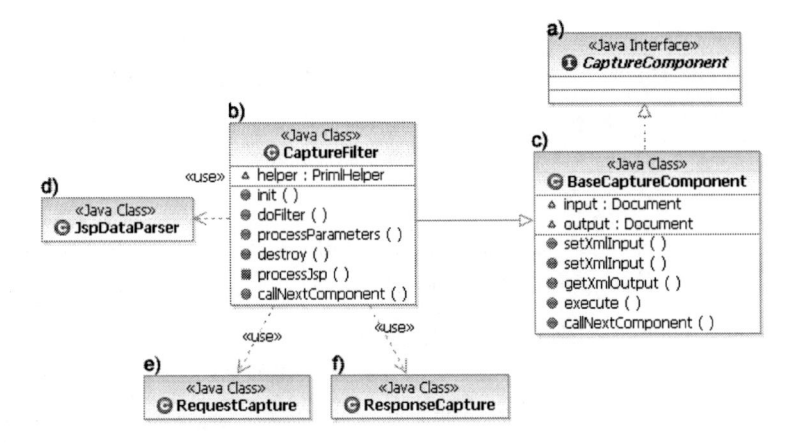

Figure 4.9: UML class dependency diagram for the capture component implementation, CaptureFilter.

The resultant IFML document is passed to the abstraction component (Figure 4.2b). In this implementation, a new IFML document is generated for every request-response; the abstraction component receives multiple IFML documents and aggregates them into a single document.

This implementation complies with the J2EE specification and can therefore be attached to all J2EE-based software applications, including any stores developed using WebSphere Commerce. For software applications not J2EE compliant, similar methods of capturing HTTP transmissions may be employed.

The UML class diagram for the implementation of the capture component is shown in Figure 4.9.

4.2.3 Abstraction component: understand information flows

The task of the abstraction component (Figure 4.2b) is to assign an abstracted data label and a level of sensitivity to a data element composed of a data descriptor and the data value. Optionally, it may group data elements with similar properties for greater simplification.

Each IFML <data> element is augmented with an abstracted data label attribute and a sensitivity attribute. The abstracted data labels are pre-determined and in this implementation are adapted from the P3P 1.1 data schema (Section 2.3.1.1). The information flow tuples remain the same ($f = \{s, d, E\}$). The set of data elements, E, is modified to consist of tuples $\{v, n, l\}$ where v and n are unchanged, and l is the new abstracted data label (v is a data value and n is the corresponding descriptor).

There are two implementations of the abstraction component, SimpleResolver (Figure 4.10c) and ComplexResolver (Figure 4.10d). The ComplexResolver is an extension of the SimpleResolver. SimpleResolver loads a mappings file that contains a listing of standard abstracted data labels and the data descriptors that may be abstracted to that particular label. Each data descriptor in the IFML document is located in the mappings file and the matching abstracted data label is added to the IFML `<data>` element as an attribute. A sample mappings file is shown in Figure 4.11. It maps the data descriptors `lastName`, `firstName`, `name`, and `personTitle` to the abstracted data label `user.name`, and maps `gender` and `userAge` to the group `user.demographics`. The XML schema document for the mappings file is in Appendix A.

The data descriptor in the mapping file can be a string or a valid Java regular expression; for example, `^.*name.*$` would match any data descriptor in the IFML document containing the text 'name'. Descriptors with no matching abstracted data label are listed and reported to the system administrator as 'unknown'; optionally, an unmatched data descriptor can generate a warning in the privacy compliance report. Each abstracted data label (`<standard>`) has a `sensitivity` attribute that gives the level of sensitivity of that piece of information on a numeric scale. In the present implementation, the level of sensitivity includes 0 (non-personal information), 1 (personal but often readily shared information), 2 (personal information often protected), 3 (sensitive personal information), and 4 (very sensitive personal information). An additional value for the level of sensitivity is `default`, which indicates that a default sensitivity level was assigned. The default sensitivity level may be configured differently for each application depending on the sensitivity of information generally handled; in our implementation, the default value is 2 (personal information).

The ComplexResolver (Figure 4.10d) implementation first uses SimpleResolver to determine if a given data descriptor exists in the mapping file. If the SimpleResolver does not return a mapping, ComplexResolver uses heuristics to automatically map the

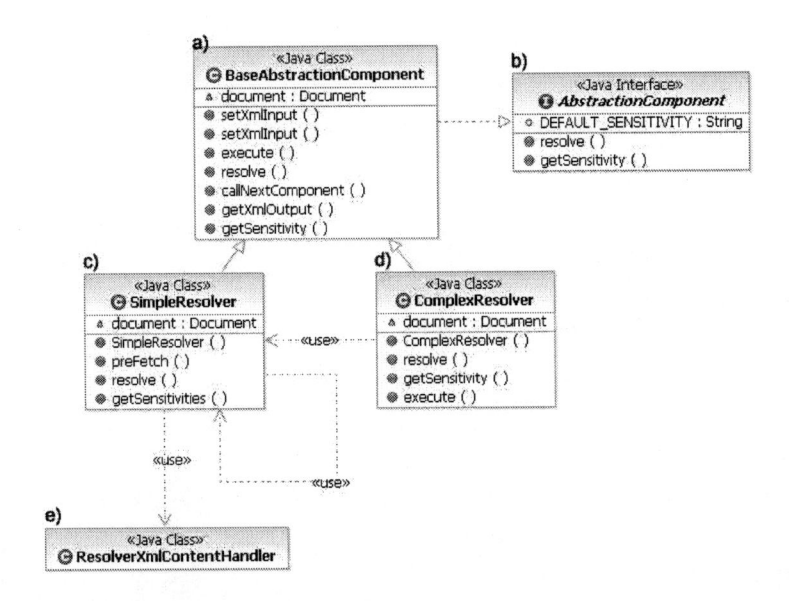

Figure 4.10: UML Class dependency diagram for the abstraction component implementations.

data descriptor to one of the standard data labels. We employ three heuristics that, although they do not necessarily identify all data descriptors, generate a mapping file compatible with SimpleResolver that can be manually modified. The three heuristics work as follows:

- **Multi-word Data Descriptors**: camelCase is a standard naming convention for variables in Java applications when the variable is a phrase. The first letter of each word in the phrase is capitalized, except for the first word (e.g., userName, aLongVariableName). Another convention is to separate multiple words with underscores (e.g., user_name, a_long_variable_name). This approach splits up multi-word data descriptors and attempts to find in the mapping XML file a mapping for each individual word. Individual words that are fewer than three characters long or that are common (e.g., 'that', 'before') are discarded (as noise words).

- **Synonym Set Mappings**: The Princeton Wordnet [30] is a lexical reference

```xml
<?xml version="1.0" encoding="UTF-8"?>
<mappings>
  <mapping>
    <standard sensitivity="1">user.name</standard>
    <descriptor>lastName</descriptor>
    <descriptor>firstName</descriptor>
    <descriptor>name</descriptor>
    <descriptor>personTitle</descriptor>
  </mapping>
  <mapping>
    <standard sensitivity="default">user.demographics</standard>
    <descriptor>gender</descriptor>
    <descriptor>userAge</descriptor>
  </mapping>
</mappings>
```

Figure 4.11: A simple XML file mapping a set of data descriptors to a single abstracted data label.

system that organizes words into *synonym sets* based on similar lexical concepts. The data descriptors, and if applicable the individual words, are looked up in a local repository of the WordNet relationships and the matching synonym set is determined. The mapping XML file is searched to determine the existence of mappings for other words in the synonym set (the file is sorted alphabetically, but in this implementation is searched in linear order). Where a word exists in more than one synonym set, the search is narrowed to synonym sets for which there are mappings. From these mappings, the mapping with the greatest level of sensitivity is chosen. For example, a Wordnet lookup of `postal_code` returns: 'ZIP code', 'ZIP', and 'postcode'.

- **Value-based Mappings**: The type of information can be determined from the data values (rather than the data descriptors like the above approaches). Some data formats are unique (eg., 111 111 111 is the format of a social insurance number); when these values appear, the abstracted data label can be guessed based on a predefined set of patterns. Additionally, when testing a software application, data entry can follow a certain pattern and enter specific values that can be uniquely identified. At present, this method is implemented using regular expressions in a mapping file.

Once the ComplexResolver has detected a mapping, it writes a mapping file in the same format as the one input by SimpleResolver; this generated mapping file may be added to the original mapping file to cache the ComplexResolver results for frequently used data descriptors. Mapping results are also cached internally; this means that if one of the above heuristics is used to determine a mapping, the mapping is stored so future lookups of the same data descriptor can be read from an XML file rather than executing each of the heuristics.

There are cases where the existing set of standard data labels to which mappings can be made automatically is not adequate to represent the information captured by the software application. In this case, the currently implemented solution is to manually add additional abstracted data labels to the mappings file based on the list of data descriptors that were not resolvable to an abstracted standard data label (one example was 'krypto', which is a special encrypted string used by IBM WebSphere Commerce). The abstraction component may attempt to group data descriptors that are not resolvable and automatically add additional standard data labels; this feature is not implemented.

The mappings file used for IBM WebSphere Commerce mapped several hundred data descriptors to an abstracted data label called "ignore" of sensitivity "0" to indicate that they did not contain personal information. Additionally, any data descriptors incorrectly abstracted by the initial execution of the ComplexResolver were included. Finally, several categories of personal information ("demographics", "financial", and "unique identifiers") were included in the mapping file.

4.2.4 Analysis component: rule evaluation

The Analysis Component (Figure 4.2d) reads a set of privacy compliance rules from an XML file and reports on the compliance of each of the flows of personal information.

The format of the rules allows tests based on the field names available in the IFML document (as defined in Section 4.2.1). Each application subset will have a set of `<source>` and `<destination>` elements; each `<source>` and `<destination>` element will have a set of `<data>` elements that have a data descriptor and an abstracted data label. For each of these data items, we also know the assigned value for the level of sensitivity and whether or not it was transmitted securely.

A privacy compliance rule is a set of compliance tuples joined by the Boolean operators AND and OR (each of equal precedence). Tuples may be nested using parentheses. A compliance tuple is of the form *(variable, operator, value[s])*. The variable is one of the seven pieces of information available in the IFML document (see Figure 4.12; for a description of the IFML elements, see Section 4.2.1). Valid operators depend on the variable type and follow the standard conventions for operators in computer programming languages. For the '!=' operator the values are a set of values this variable may not be; for the '==' operator the values are a set of values of which the variable must equal one. For more examples, see Table 4.4.

Only a single compliance tuple is necessary to make a complete rule. If a variable is not in the rule, its value does not matter. The "Any" operator provides a way to state this explicitly. The set of variables, the set of valid operators, and the set of valid value(s) are listed in Figure 4.12.

Each of the compliance tuples resolves to a boolean value (true or false); the various ANDs and ORs determine the final result of the rule (again, true or false). A rule with a final result of 'true' is said to have passed; otherwise, assertion of the rule is said to have failed and the appropriate entry ('warning', 'error', or 'unknown') is made in the IFML document.

The rules derived in Section 4.1 from privacy legislation and privacy policies were translated into the rule format required by the Analysis Component. The translation for a set of exemplar rules is shown in Table 4.4.

Variable	Valid Operators	Content of Values (Example)
Subset	Any	Empty (Subset, Any)
	==	Set of values Subset may be (Subset, ==, "UserLogin,UserRegistration")
	!=	Set of values Subset must not be (Subset, !=, "DrawInterface")
Source	Any	Empty (Source, Any)
	==	Set of values Source may be (Source, ==, "User, Cookie")
	!=	Set of values Source must not be (Source, !=, "URL")
Destination	Any	Empty (Destination, Any)
	==	Set of values Destination may be (Destination, ==, "User, Cookie")
	!=	Set of values Destination must not be (Destination, !=, "URL")
Data Descriptor (DD)	Any	Empty (DD, Any)
	==	Set of values DD may be (DD, ==, "user.creditcard")
	!=	Set of values DD must not be (DD, !=, "user.non-personal, user.ignore")
Abstracted Data Label (ADL)	Any	Empty (ADL, Any)
	==	Set of values DD may be (ADL, ==, "user.creditcard")
	!=	Set of values DD must not be (ADL, !=, "user.non-personal, user.ignore")
	Unresolvable	'1' or '0' (ADL, Unresolvable, '1')
Sensitivity	==	A single numeric value (Sensitivity, ==, 1)
	!=	A single numeric value (Sensitivity, !=, 0)
	>, >=	A single numeric value (Sensitivity, >=, 1)
	<, <=	(Sensitivity, <=, 3)
Encrypted	==	'1' or '0' (Encrypted, ==, 1)

Figure 4.12: The variables, operators, and values that make up compliance tuples for the rule-based analysis.

Original	Sensitive information must be encrypted during transmission (Table 4.1)
Translated	(Sensitivity,<, 2) OR (Encrypted, ==, 1)
Original	Information in the cookies or the URL must be encrypted during transmission (Table 4.1)
Translated	(Sensitivity,<, 1) OR (Encrypted, ==, 1) OR ((Source, !=, [Cookie, URL]) AND (Destination, !=, [Cookie, URL]))
Original	The Social Insurance Number or Social Security Number must not be collected (Table 4.1)
Translated	(Abstracted Data Label, !=, SIN)
Original	No personal information may be collected. (Table 4.3)
Translated	(Sensitivity,<, 1)
Original	Information may not be sent to any entity other than a delivery agent. (Table 4.3)
Translated	(Sensitivity,<, 1) OR (Destination, ==, [Delivery, User, Cookie, URL])
Original	Information may not be sent to any third parties. (Table 4.3)
Translated	(Sensitivity,<, 1) OR (Destination, ==, [User, Cookie, URL])

Table 4.4: Exemplar rules translated from the legislative rules (Table 4.1) and the P3P rules (Table 4.3).

The analysis component reads the IFML document. The rules are sorted according to which level of the IFML document they apply. Those rules that apply only to top-level elements are assigned to a group, rules that apply only to the next level of elements are assigned to a group, and so on. The top-level element rules are assessed each time an <application_subset> element is encountered. The next-level element rules are assessed each time a <source> or <destination> element is encountered. The final element rules are assessed each time a <data> element is encountered. The result of each rule assessment is written to the IFML document using the <rule> element.

A rule is evaluated by evaluating each of the compliance tuples and replacing the compliance tuple in the rule with the appropriate boolean value, either true or false. The AND and OR operators are converted to the Java && and || operators, respectively. The parentheses are not modified. The modified rule is evaluated as a Java expression, and the resulting value (true or false) is the result of the rule.

A SimpleRuleBasedAnalysisComponent class is implemented to handle the rule-based analysis. The UML class diagram of the current implementation is shown in Figure 4.13.

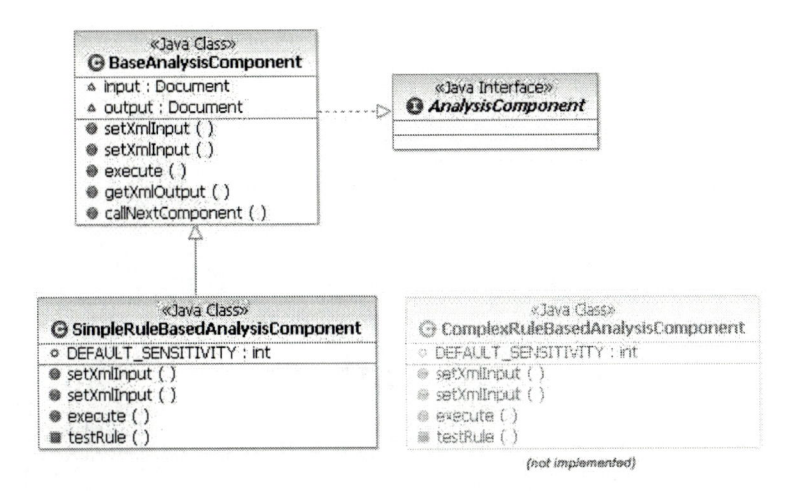

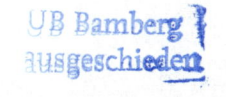

Figure 4.13: The UML class dependency diagram for the analysis component.

4.2.5 Display component: report on compliance

The Display Component (Figure 4.2e) converts the IFML document to a human-readable document. Multiple reports may be generated with different levels of detail. It can be executed at the same time as the rest of the privacy compliance testing components, or separately. It may be run once, or run multiple times with different parameters to generate different reports. There are two different implementations of the display component, either of which can be used. Our testing used the XML Transformation display component. The UML class diagram is shown in Figure 4.14.

4.2.5.1 XML transformations

This implementation (called XslDisplayComponent, Figure 4.14b) uses XML transformations to transform the IFML document into an HTML document that can be displayed by a web browser. XML Transformations [135] are part of the eXtensible

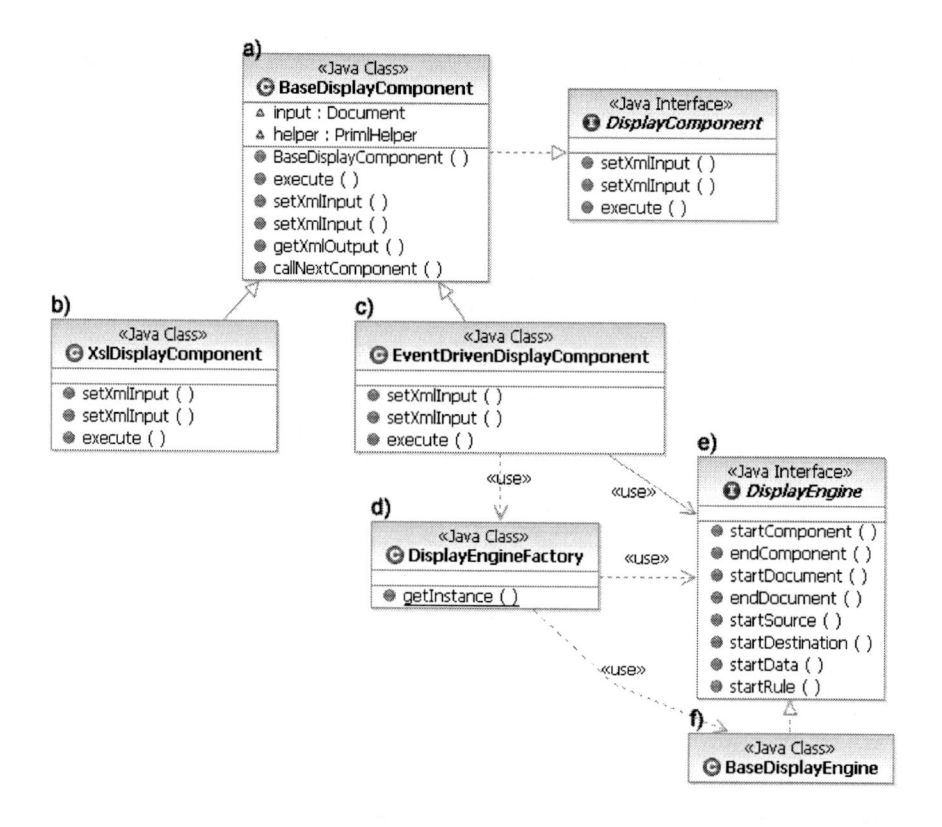

Figure 4.14: The UML class dependency diagram for the display component.

Stylesheet Language (XSL) family [134], a set of W3C recommendations for determining how to display and process XML documents. An eXtensible Stylesheet Language Transformation (XSLT) file contains rules for transforming an XML document into other text-based documents, including plain text files, HTML, or XML documents with different structure. This implementation uses XSLT to generate a set of navigable HTML documents from the IFML report.

The XslDisplayComponent applies an XSL stylesheet to the IFML document and stores the results in a set of HTML files. To decrease the time required to load the documents when viewed by humans, it uses the XSL implementation [14] from Apache to do the transformation at program run time, rather than doing it dynamically every time the IFML file is opened in the browser. The implementation is passed the name of an XSL stylesheet, which means multiple XSL files can be defined so this one implementation can be used to generate multiple views. The XslDisplayComponent can apply the XSL file to the entire IFML document and save it to a file or it can iteratively apply the stylesheet to each `<application_subset>` in the IFML file and write the output to a unique file name.

Three stylesheets are used in this implementation:

1. individual.xsl: Generates a detailed view for each application subset, each being stored in a separate HTML file. The view includes a graphic depiction of the information flow and a listing of the rules that failed, including for each the rule name, rule outcome, and rule message (Figure 4.15). This document is included in Appendix B.3.

UserRegistrationAdd

Information Flow

user → password, password, shoppingpattern, user.uniqueId, demographics, email, user.preferences, unknown.unknown, server.ignore → Application → shoppingpattern, demographics, user.preferences, server.ignore → user

URL → shoppingpattern, demographics, user.preferences → Application → shoppingpattern, demographics, user.preferences → URL

Rule-based Analysis

Name	Result	Message
Secure Transmission	fail	Sensitive information password sent unsecured from User.
URL	fail	Personal information included in the URL.
Unidentified	warning	Some application-specific information could not be resolved.

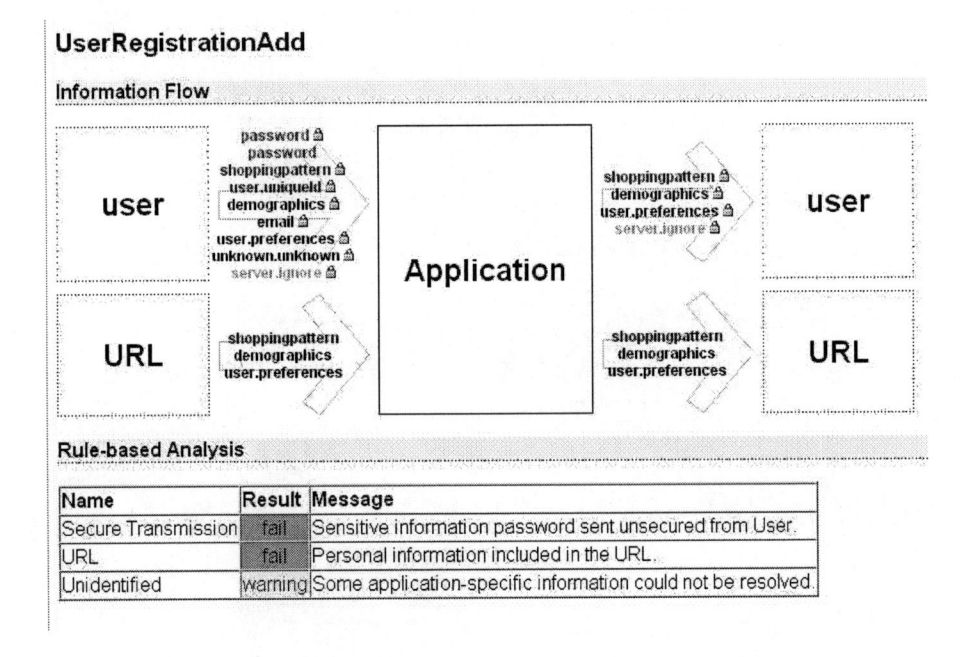

Figure 4.15: Sample output from the individual.xsl XML transformation to HTML, after rendering.

2. overview.xsl: Generates a listing of all the application subsets on a single page,

with red bars indicating failures and a list of what rules cause the failure point (Figure 4.16). This document is included in Appendix B.1.

3. detailed-overview.xsl: Generates a list of all the application subsets on a single page, and for each application subset gives the rule tested, the outcome, and the message (Figure 4.17). This document is included in Appendix B.2.

Overview

UserRegistrationAdd	Secure Transmission	URL	Unidentified
TopCategoriesDisplay		Sensitive information password sent unsecured from User.	
LogonForm			
LogonForm			
UserRegistrationForm			
OrderItemDisplay			
CategoryDisplay			

Figure 4.16: Sample output from the overview.xsl XML transformation to HTML, after rendering.

Detailed Overview

Component: UserRegistrationAdd

Name	Result	Message
Secure Transmission	fail	Sensitive information password sent unsecured from User.
URL	fail	Personal information included in the URL.
Unidentified	warning	Some application-specific information could not be resolved.

Component: TopCategoriesDisplay

Name	Result	Message

Figure 4.17: Sample output from the detailed-overview.xsl XML transformation to HTML, after rendering.

4.2.5.2 SAX-like parsing

The *de facto* standard for XML processing in Java is the Simple API for XML (SAX). The basic SAX model is to have a parser read the XML file and to issue events when certain conditions are met (e.g., reached a new element, reached the end of an element, reached a comment, etc.). Programs using a SAX parser can listen for these events and act based on the events issued by a SAX processors [103].

This implementation of the display component, called the EventDrivenDisplayComponent (Figure 4.14c), uses a similar model. It takes as a parameter an object that wishes to listen for events and that implements the DisplayEngine interface (called the 'display engine'), Figure 4.14e. It processes the XML document and sends events to the display engine each time a new IFML element is reached. The display engine uses these events to generate a display. In the analogy to the SAX XML parser, the DisplayEngine is the handler and the EventDrivenDisplayComponent is the DocumentBuilder.

The EventDrivenDisplayComponent is implemented (Figure 4.14c), the DisplayEngine interface is specified (Figure 4.14e), the DisplayEngineFactory which locates and returns a class that implements the DisplayEngine interface is implemented (Figure 4.14d), but only a basic display engine (BaseDisplayEngine) not capable of generating views is implemented (Figure 4.14f).

4.3 Privacy Compliance Testing Results

The proof-of-concept implementation of privacy compliance testing was applied to a sample electronic commerce store provided with IBM WebSphere Commerce and tested. This section presents the results.

4.3.1 Test environment

The IBM WebSphere Commerce implementation of the privacy compliance testing methodology was tested on two versions of IBM WebSphere Commerce running on two different test machines:

- **IBM WebSphere Commerce 6.0** (pre-release development build [September 13 2005], developer edition, full source code available): Windows 2000, 1280 MB RAM, Pentium 4, Cloudscape database, Java Development Kit 1.4.2, running in Rational Application Developer test environment. Sample Store: ConsumerDirect.

- **IBM WebSphere Commerce 5.6.1** (commercial release, developer edition, no source code available): Windows XP, 1024 MB RAM, Pentium 4, Cloudscape database, Java Development Kit 1.4.1, running in IBM WebSphere Application Developer 5.1.2 test environment. Sample Store: ConsumerDirect.

When applicable, individual components were tested in a different test platform without IBM WebSphere Commerce. This test machine had Windows XP, 1024 MB RAM, Pentium M 1.6 GHz, and all power settings on maximum.

4.3.2 Testing information flows

The proof-of-concept implementation of the privacy compliance testing application was deployed to the sample retailer (using their sample store, ConsumerDirect, which is included with IBM WebSphere Commerce as a starting point for real-world retailers). It is a fully functioning retailer. Initial tests were run on the unmodified sample retailer, and no non-compliant information flows were discovered. Manual assessment of the sample retailer did not locate non-compliant information flows. We altered the sample retailer to simulate the changes a real-world retailer might make when developing their own e-commerce store.

The rules enforced by the current implementation, and the modifications made to the sample retailer included with IBM WebSphere Commerce to trigger these rules are listed in Table 4.5. These are drawn from Table 4.4 based on the P3P version of the privacy policy shipped with the sample store [104].

For simplicity, our privacy compliance testing assumed that the abstraction component mapping file was configured to accurately classify all of the information transmitted by the application. This state of accurate classification is achievable in practice. This state was ensured for the portions of the application to which privacy violations were introduced as suggested by an individual familiar with privacy and WebSphere Commerce but not involved in developing this implementation. The implementation detected 100% of the non-compliant information flows. A false detection of non-compliance was generated when the form requested personal information (social insurance number) but the user entered non-personal information (the string "will not disclose"). The abstraction component classifies data elements based on what the

Rule	Sensitive information must be encrypted during transmission
Test	Modify the user registration page to submit using HTTP instead of HTTPs
Rule	Information in the cookies or the URL must be encrypted during transmission
Test	Include sensitive information as parameters in the URL of the request
Rule	The Social Insurance Number or Social Security Number must not be collected
Test	Modify the user registration page to request a social insurance number
Rule	Passwords should not be sent to the user
Test	Modify the user registration page to confirm a user's password by displaying it
Rule	An individual should be the sole source of personal information about himself or herself
Test	Personal information that the user did not submit is sent to the user

Table 4.5: The rules enforced by this implementation and the tests used to verify violations can be detected.

application requested, not what the user provided.

This set of rules is not sufficiently large to obtain an accurate false-positive/false-negative rate. When testing for privacy compliance in a development environment, false detections of privacy non-compliance are preferred to missed detections. Thus, our implementation was designed to be conservative and report non-compliance if the results were unclear.

We conclude that our implementation is capable of detecting non-compliant information flows. However, further testing should test information flows from an application with a known but naturally-occurring non-compliant information flow.

Our proof-of-concept implementation is limited by only capturing information flows from or to the customer. The number of rules that can be enforced on only these information flows is limited.

4.3.3 Performance of privacy compliance testing

Performance is not our primary metric for this implementation, since privacy compliance testing may be implemented in a test environment and not used in the production environment, and since in our case it was implemented in a proof-of-concept environment. However, the performance of the implementation is still relevant due to increased response time when the capture component is implemented as a filter. The primary purpose of the IBM WebSphere Commerce application is to receive requests, process them, and return a response to the client. The time that elapses between when a client submits a request and when a client receives the complete response is called the *response time*. Introducing a filter between the client and the software application increases the response time.

The capture component (a J2EE filter) captures requests and responses in memory. The response is returned to the client before the IFML document is saved to persistent storage. This reduces the effect on the response time. The abstraction, analysis, and display components need only run after a sufficient number of information flows have been captured and can be run on a separate machine; however, if the components and the IBM WebSphere Commerce application execute on the machine, response time for requests will increase while the components are executing. Running some components on separate machines also precludes analyzing flows in real-time and stopping transactions when non-compliant flows are protected.

To test capture component performance, response time (from when the application received a request to when the application sent back the response) was measured with the capture component filter present versus with the capture component filter absent for three different tasks. The results are in Table 4.6.

To test the performance of the remaining components, IFML files were randomly generated based on numbers chosen based on IFML generated when testing using WebSphere Commerce. Each `<application_subset>` element has 12 +/- 2 sources and 12 +/- 2 destinations. Each source and destination has 104 +/- 20 `<data>` elements. Each element had all of its attributes. The 1 MB file had 11 `<application_subset>` elements, the 10 MB file had 100, the 25 MB file had 250, and the 50 MB file had 500. The number of `<data>` elements in each file is given in

Table 4.7.

The performance of the analysis component was tested with an IFML file 1MB in size; with only five rules to compare, execution time was under 200 milliseconds. This execution time is negligible compared to the other components.

The performance of the abstraction component was tested by processing each of the randomly generated IFML files and calculating the rate at which data descriptors could be converted into abstracted data labels by the SimpleResolver using an XML mapping file. The time elapsed while executing (excluding the time spent reading the file) is shown in Table 4.7.

	Login	Add User	View Catalog
Execution time without filter (ms)	135	74	80
Execution time with filter (ms)	156	89	94
Difference (ms)	21	15	14
Difference (%)	16%	20%	18%

Table 4.6: The response time of the web application for three tasks, with and without a filter.

File Size	# of Data Descriptors	Running Time (s)
1 MB	22,172	0.3
10 MB	213,396	1.0
25 MB	513,674	19.9
50 MB	1,038,978	170.9

Table 4.7: The running times of the abstraction component for IFML documents of varying size and the number of unique lookups required.

The performance of the display component was tested using the randomly generated IFML files. We measured the time required by the XslDisplayComponent to generate all three XSL views in static HTML and save them to disk. The running time (excluding the time spent reading the IFML file but including the time spent writing the HTML files) is shown in Table 4.8. The performance of Apache implementation of XSL transformations degrades for XML files larger than 25 MB.

The current implementation of the components loads the entire IFML document into memory. The Document Object Model (DOM) creates a Java object for each

File Size	Running Time (s)
1 MB	6.1
10 MB	22.5
25 MB	168.9
50 MB	3904.5

Table 4.8: The running times of the display component for IFML documents of varying size.

XML element in the file. Performance degrades for IFML files larger than 50MB, though that limit varies based on the content of the IFML file.

Performance of the capture component is acceptable. A production implementation would have improved performance and less impact on response time. Any response time impact might be unacceptable, but a 5% increase in response time can be compensated for. Performance of the other components degrades as the IFML file increases in size; however, IFML file size will be limited by the size of the application and the number of unique information flows and we expect this file size will not exceed the point where performance degrades. If ever run in a production environment, the other components should be executed on a separate server and performance should be a consideration when implementing these components. The response time performance is not relevant in a testing environment. The current implementation is scalable up to a certain number of unique data descriptors (approximately 500,000).

4.3.4 Extensibility of the implementation

The current implementation is readily extensible to capture information flows from sources other than the user, to use additional mappings, to compare additional rules, and to generate different views. The component-based architecture with defined Java interfaces dictating the behavior of components allows for existing components to be extended or replaced with alternate implementations, without modifying components for which functionality need not be updated. The IFML specification is designed to handle general cases and general components; however, if the IFML schema must be modified, the helper object used by the current implementation can be modified to write to the new schema without modifying the existing components.

The implementation allows for any number of capture components. Capturing information flows from other sources requires writing a component to capture the information flow and sending the resultant IFML file to the existing abstraction component.

The existing abstraction component can be improved by editing the mapping file to include explicit mappings between data descriptors and abstracted data labels and by creating additional regular expressions. The analysis component can be improved by adding additional rules to the rules file. The display component can be expanded by creating additional XSL files to generate views or by implementing a display engine for fine-tuned control when traversing IFML files.

4.4 Summary

In this chapter, we described proof-of-concept implementations of two modules of our enterprise privacy policy management framework.

In our privacy policy creation module, we combined policy elements from two important policy resources: privacy legislation and the enterprise's own privacy promises as expressed in their P3P policy. We created policy rules of a sample privacy policy with the intent of demonstrating that our proposed methodology for policy creation would be effective.

Our proof-of-concept implementation of a software application for privacy policy compliance included modular components, each of which provided one part of the functionality described in the methodology. The components communicate using an XML-based language created for the purpose. The capture component captures information flows between the customer (client) and the application (server). The abstraction component converts these information flows to a standard set of abstracted data labels. The analysis component compares the information flows to a set of rules. The display component generates HTML files from the privacy compliance report, giving three different views based on three different stylesheets. This implementation was capable of detecting information flows that were non-compliant with performance that is suitable for a test environment.

Chapter 5

Conclusion

Information system privacy (and security) are important to society at large. The challenges and requirements demand new approaches from technology [75]. Of security and privacy, security has attracted more attention from researchers in North America and Europe. However, protecting personal privacy is critical to the success of a knowledge economy. Each individual should have the freedom to choose who may collect his or her personal information and what they may do with it once it is collected.

As electronic commerce retailers collect, store, and use increasing amounts of personal information, technology, the law, individuals, and the retailers themselves must address the issue of individual privacy. Consumers are concerned about their privacy, and this concern is a barrier to the continued growth of electronic commerce. Governments are paying close attention to the privacy of personal information, and countries including Canada and the member countries of the European Union have passed broad privacy legislation. Businesses, in response to the concerns of consumers and legislators, have begun to address privacy in their business processes and software.

At present, there are ways to express privacy policies to consumers (P3P) and internally (EPAL), but our literature search did not reveal a systematic approach to determining an enterprise privacy policy based on the requirements and influences of a set of policy resources.

The state-of-the-art in enforcing privacy policy on an enterprise's employees, business processes, and software and testing for compliance with a privacy policy includes educating employees and conducting manual privacy impact assessments to determine potential privacy violations in business processes. These assessments do not consider the software in detail; it is one more item on a manual checklist. Solutions that involve creating access controls from a written privacy policy address only one aspect of the privacy of software applications. Security threat models have been developed to assess the security threats to a software application, and researchers have done work on similar models for privacy in ubiquitous computing. These models are manual surveys, and the existing privacy models are focused on ubiquitous computing and address the design phase of software, not testing an existing application for privacy compliance.

In our research, we focused on a general framework for enterprise privacy policy management. Based on an informal description of the framework, we defined a software framework and its requirements. The framework includes modules responsible for creating, deploying, validating/verifying, enforcing, and testing for compliance with an enterprise privacy policy. The framework is readily extensible; it was designed to be incrementally developed as the details of the privacy challenge emerge and as the challenge evolves over time. This framework co-exists with existing software applications; it is a layer between the middleware and the software applications and can be considered as an extension of the middleware. We expect that this new privacy layer will not require the modification of existing software applications.

To demonstrate the feasibility of this informal framework, we defined and implemented two of the modules, privacy policy creation and privacy policy compliance testing.

To create a policy, we defined the set of privacy policy resources. We defined the properties of a privacy policy resource, its privacy policy, and the elements of that privacy policy. Using this representation, we proposed a process for determining a set of privacy policies that applied to the enterprise and each of its component retailers. We chose the two most important policy resources and combined their privacy requirements into a single sample enterprise privacy policy. Canadian privacy legislation was one policy resource; the other was the enterprise's own privacy commitments as expressed in their P3P policy. We successfully represented each set of privacy policy requirements as a set of rules and combined them to form a single enterprise privacy policy. This approach can be easily extended to include other legislation and other policy resources.

To test a software application for compliance with an enterprise privacy policy, we proposed the privacy compliance testing methodology. We modified the existing e-commerce workflows (as originally defined by IBM) to include privacy monitors (filters). Each privacy filter monitors the information flows that support the workflow by capturing them and converting the application-specific flows into a standardized representation based on pre-defined data types. These flows are tested for compliance with a set of privacy rules. The monitor can execute a variety of actions when detecting non-compliant information flows, including warning the customer, notifying the administrator, or holding or canceling the transaction. This approach does not require any modification of existing software applications, which makes it more economically practical for an enterprise to deploy. Although tested in the sector of electronic commerce, we believe this approach will be applicable to software in other sectors of the economy such as e-health.

A proof-of-concept implementation of privacy compliance testing was developed and deployed to a leading electronic commerce software application, IBM WebSphere Commerce. To test the methodology in real-world conditions, the application source code was not modified. We successfully captured information flows between the customer and the application, represented them using standardized data types, and detected information flows that did not comply with our set of privacy policy rules. The implementation is easily extensible to test for compliance with additional rules or use different standardized data types without modifying the source code. Implementing additional capture components will allow the capture of additional information flows, and any of the components of our implementation can be readily replaced or extended without modifying the other components.

The development and testing of the privacy compliance testing methodology was conducted in collaboration with IBM. The privacy compliance testing methodology is one approach a software vendor may use to test their software for compliance with privacy legislation. Our description of the methodology did not explicitly address this use of our implementation. However, our unique methodology has been submitted for a joint patent with several IBM employees, and our proof-of-concept implementation was used to identify potential privacy compliance issues to a software development team.

Ultimately, we have demonstrated that we can test a software application for compliance with a defined set of privacy policy rules. Though not a complete solution, this beginning demonstrates that privacy management in technology is not an impossible question. The answer to privacy is not "You have none. Get over it." With appropriate legislation, demand from individuals, and support from businesses, technology can address the issue of privacy.

5.1 Hypotheses

Hypothesis 1 stated that "The entities that influence an e-commerce retailer's privacy policy can be identified, represented and used to determine the retailer's privacy policy as a set of structured privacy policy rules."

While we are not able to accept or reject Hypothesis 1, we provided evidence in support of it. We developed the methodology, identified two policy resources, defined a sample set of privacy policy elements for each, and combined the sets into a sample enterprise privacy policy. This limited experiment demonstrates the feasibility of this approach, but does not sufficiently demonstrate that our proposed approach can identify and represent all of the possible policy resources, nor does it establish that an e-commerce retailer's privacy policy can be expressed in the form of structured privacy policy rules. The methodology was effective for our limited experiment and we believe that further implementation work will demonstrate the validity of this hypothesis.

Hypothesis 2 stated that "It can be verified that the communications between an e-commerce retailer's software application and the retailer's consumers comply with a set of privacy policy rules."

We accept this hypothesis. We represented the communication between a retailer and its customers as a set of information flows that follow a defined workflow, defined a methodology, and implemented an application capable of capturing these information flows and determining if they complied with a sample set of privacy policy rules. This proof-of-concept implementation demonstrates the validity of our hypothesis.

5.2 Future Work

This work described a methodology and software framework for managing enterprise privacy policy management, including creation, deployment, validation, verification, and enforcement. This framework was not fully implemented, although a proof-of-concept policy was created. Future work will implement this framework and demonstrate the validity of our proposed approach. This demonstration will address the outstanding requirements to accept Hypothesis 1. The framework was designed using an incremental approach; this future work is the next iteration of development. This iteration will include a formal description of the framework, which may include revisions to enable a formal representation.

The current proof-of-concept privacy compliance testing implementation captures information sent between the user and the software application. It has been designed so that additional information flows can be captured without modifying the rest of the implementation. One extension would be to capture information as it is stored to or retrieved from the database, or to filter information

This work does not specifically address the issue of risk in privacy compliance testing. We believe that like in software testing, privacy compliance testing is an exercise in risk management. It cannot provide guarantees, but we can identify high-risk subsets of the software application. Additionally, any detections of non-compliance should be risk assessed, similar to a mechanism used in a security threat model (but automatically). Future work should investigate the relation of risk to privacy compliance testing and how to manage privacy in a cost-effective manner.

We attempted to automatically extract privacy policy rules from legislation documents, but this problem was out of the scope of this research. An enhancement to our approach of manually extracting privacy policy rules would be augmenting this manual analysis with software that identifies key sections and phrases and converts them into our rule format. The policy expert could identify additional phrases for which the software would generate a suggested conversion into the privacy policy rule format.

When combining policy resource privacy policies into an overall enterprise privacy policy and a set of retailer privacy policies, there may be policy conflicts that must be resolved in the policy creation process. The current methodology recognizes that this must be addressed but does not describe a mechanism for automatically doing so. Existing research in policy formulation can be extended to address policy conflict in privacy policies and automatically detect and resolve these conflicts.

At present, the privacy compliance testing methodology describes enhancing workflows to include privacy monitoring and taking action based on this monitoring. Our proof-of-concept implementation monitors the flows of information that follow the workflow, but the only action is to generate a report that can be used to resolve the compliance issue. The implementation is intended to operate in the test environment. A next step would be to deploy privacy monitoring in a production environment and to enable the privacy monitor to stop transactions or warn the customer before continuing. This would require a study of the workflows to determine the optimal positioning of a privacy monitor. A further step would include modifying the software or the software's configuration automatically at runtime to correct privacy compliance issues. Future work could consider whether or not informing a customer if an information flow is compliant or non-compliant with a privacy policy would increase their trust for the online store.

This research focused on retailers engaged in electronic commerce and the software applications they employ. We believe the methodologies presented herein are appropriate for other sectors of the e-economy, such as e-banking, e-government, or e-health, but do not address these sectors. An examination of these sectors and the challenges to our methodology must address to be appropriate to these sectors would be a useful generalization of the current research.

Our representation of the set of policy resources included properties and software modules for localization, language, and cultural factors. We have not verified that these properties are sufficient to represent this aspect of privacy. One line of research would employ our methodology to represent policy resources from different countries and cultures.

Bibliography

[1] *The Oxford English Dictionary.* "e-commerce". Oxford University Press, 2nd edition, 1989.

[2] *The Oxford English Dictionary.* "privacy". Oxford University Press, 2nd edition, 1989.

[3] *Family Education Rights Privacy Act* (United States of America), 20 U.S.C. § 1232g; P.L. 93-380, 1974. Approved 1974.

[4] *Privacy Act* (United States of America), 5 U.S.C. § 552a; P.L. 93-579, 1974. Approved 1974.

[5] *Video Privacy Protection Act* (United States of America), 18 U.S.C. § 2710; P.L. 100-618, 1974. Approved 1974.

[6] *Children's Online Privacy Protection Act* (United States of America), 15 U.S.C. § 6501; P.L. 105-277, 1998. Approved 1998.

[7] *Personal Information Protection and Electronic Documents Act* (Canada), Second Session, Thirty-sixth Parliament, 48-49 Elizabeth II, 1999-2000. Assented to April 2000.

[8] *Privacy Act* (Canada), First Session, Thirty-second Parliament, 29-30-31-32 Elizabeth II, 1980-1983. Assented to June 1983.

[9] Department of Human Resources and Social Development (Canada). Authorized uses of the social insurance number (SIN), last visited June 2006. `http://www.hrsdc.gc.ca/asp/gateway.asp?hr=/en/cs/sin/075.shtml&hs=sxn`.

[10] Philip E. Agre and Marc Rotenberg (editors). *Technology and Privacy: The New Landscape.* MIT Press, 1997.

[11] Irving Altman. Privacy regulation: Culturally universal or culturally specific? *Journal of Social Issues*, 33(3):66–84, 1977.

[12] Daniel Amor. *The E-business (R)Evolution: Living and Working In An Interconnected World.* Prentice Hall PTR, 2001.

[13] Robert C. Angell. Preferences for moral norms in three problem areas. *The American Journal of Sociology*, 67(6):650–660, May 1962.

[14] Apache XML Project. Xalan-java version 2.7.0, last visited November 2005. `http://xml.apache.org/xalan-j/`.

[15] Art Technology Group. ATG Commerce, last visited April 2006. http://www.atg.com/en/products/ecommerce/commerce.jhtml.

[16] Gary Bahadur, William Chan, and Chris Weber. *Privacy Defended: Protecting Yourself Online*, chapter 3, "Privacy Organizations and Initiatives". Que, 2002.

[17] Katrina Baum. Identity theft 2004. Department of Justice Bureau of Statistics, NCJ 212213, April 2006. http://www.ojp.usdoj.gov/bjs/abstract/it04.htm.

[18] Boris Beizer. *Software system testing and quality assurance.* Van Nostrand Reinhold Company, Inc, 1984.

[19] Brian Bergstein. Visa, Amex cut ties with card processor. Associated Press, via USA Today, July 20, 2005. http://www.usatoday.com/tech/techinvestor/corporatenews/2005-07-20-visa-amex-cut-ties_x.htm.

[20] Louis Brandeis and Samuel Warren. The right to privacy. *Harvard Law Review*, IV(5):193–220, 1890.

[21] David Brin. *The Transparent Society: Will Technology Force Us to Choose Between Privacy and Freedom?* Perseus Books Group, 1999.

[22] California Office of Privacy Protection. Privacy laws, last updated February 2006. http://www.privacy.ca.gov/lawenforcement/laws.htm.

[23] Canadian Medical Association. Health information privacy code, 1998. http://www.cma.ca/index.cfm/ci_id/3216/la_id/1.htm.

[24] Canadian Standards Association. Model code for the protection of personal information, March 1996.

[25] Center for Democracy and Technology. Online banking privacy: A slow, confusing start to giving customers control over their information, 2001. http://www.cdt.org/privacy/financial/010829onlinebanking.pdf.

[26] Center for Democracy and Technology. Digital search & seizure: Updating privacy protections to keep pace with technology, February 2006. http://www.cdt.org/publications/digital-search-and-seizure.pdf.

[27] Center for Democracy and Technology and the Information and Privacy Commissioner of Ontario. P3P and privacy: An update for the privacy community, March 2000. http://www.cdt.org/privacy/pet/p3pprivacy.shtml.

[28] Angela Choy and Janlori Goldman. Comparing eHealth privacy initiatives. Prepared for the California HealthCare Foundation, 2001. http://www.chcf.org/topics/view.cfm?itemID=12739.

[29] CNN.com. Privacy groups debate DoubleClick settlement, May 24, 2002. http://archives.cnn.com/2002/TECH/internet/05/24/doubleclick.settlement.idg/.

[30] Princeton University Cognitive Science Laboratory. Wordnet, a lexical database for the english language, 2006. http://wordnet.princeton.edu/.

[31] Karen Coyle. P3P: Pretty poor privacy?, 1999. http://www.kcoyle.net/p3p.html.

[32] Lorrie Cranor. P3P and privacy on the web FAQ. World Wide Web Consortium, 2002. http://www.w3.org/P3P/p3pfaq.html.

[33] Lorrie Faith Cranor. *Privacy and Self-Regulation in the Information Age*, chapter 3, "The Role of Technology in Self-Regulatory Privacy Regimes". U.S. Department of Commerce, National Telecommunications and Information Administration, 1997. http://www.ntia.doc.gov/reports/privacy/privacy_rpt.htm.

[34] Mary J Culnan and Pamela K Armstrong. Information privacy concerns, procedural fairness, and impersonal trust: An empirical investigation. *Organization Science*, 10(1):104–115, 1999.

[35] Customer Respect Group. Customer Respect Group 2005 privacy report on how corporations treat online customers, 2005. http://www.customerrespect.com/default.asp?hdnFileID=10.

[36] Department of Justice (Canada). Access to information and privacy: Canadian provinces and territories, last updated February 2006. http://www.justice.gc.ca/en/ps/atip/provte.html.

[37] Peter Drucker. *Guidelines to Our changing Society*, chapter 2, "The Age of Discontinuity". ISBN 0465089844. Harper and Row, New York, NY, 1969.

[38] ebusinessforum.com. emarketer: The great online privacy debate, 2000. http://www.ebusinessforum.com/index.asp?doc_id=1785&layout=rich_story.

[39] Electronic Privacy Information Center. Pretty poor privacy: An assessment of P3P and internet privacy, June 2000. http://www.epic.org/reports/prettypoorprivacy.html.

[40] Electronic Privacy Information Center. EPIC online guide to practical privacy tools, last updated February 2006. http://www.epic.org/privacy/tools.html.

[41] Electronic Privacy Information Center, last visited April 2006. http://www.epic.org/.

[42] Electronic Privacy Information Center and Privacy International. Privacy and human rights 2004: An international survey of privacy laws and developments, 2004. http://www.privacyinternational.org/survey/.

[43] Ernst & Young. Assurance and advisory business services - technology and security risk services - services - privacy advisory services, last visited May 2006. http://www.ey.com/global/content.nsf/US/AABS_-_TSRS_-_Services_-_Privacy.

[44] European Commission. Status of implementation of directive 95/46, 2006. http://europa.eu.int/comm/justice_home/fsj/privacy/law/implementation_en.htm.

[45] European Parliament. Directive 95/46/EC of the European Parliament and of the Council of 24 October 1995 on the protection of individuals with regard to the processing of personal data and on the free movement of such data, October 1995.

[46] European Parliament. Directive 2002/58/EC of the European Parliament and of the Council of 12 July 2002 concerning the processing of personal data and the protection of privacy in the electronic communications sector (directive on privacy and electronic communications), July 2002.

[47] Federal Trade Commission. Self-regulation and privacy online: a report to Congress. Washington, DC, July 1999.

[48] Federal Trade Commission. Privacy online: Fair information practices in the electronic marketplace, 2000. http://www.ftc.gov/reports/privacy2000/privacy2000.pdf.

[49] Federal Trade Commission. UMG Recordings, Inc. to pay $400,000, Bonzi Software, Inc. to pay $75,000 to settle COPPA civil penalty charges, February 2004. http://www.ftc.gov/opa/2004/02/bonziumg.htm.

[50] Simson Garfinkel. *Database Nation : The Death of Privacy in the 21st Century*. O'Reilly Media, Inc., 2001.

[51] Beth Givens. Identity theft: How it happens, its impact on victims, and legislative solutions. Privacy Rights Clearinghouse, Written Testimony for U.S. Senate Judiciary Subcommittee on Technology, Terrorism, and Government Information, last updated July 2000. http://www.privacyrights.org/ar/id_theft.htm.

[52] Eric Goldman. Does online privacy 'really' matter?, 2003. Available:http://www.circleid.com/article/250_0_1_0_C/.

[53] Jim Harper. Privacy: A right? or something else? Privacilla.org, 2002. http://www.privacilla.org/fundamentals/privacyright.html.

[54] Harris Interactive. First major post-9.11 privacy survey finds consumers demanding companies do more to protect privacy; public wants company privacy policies to be independently verified, 2002. http://www.harrisinteractive.com/news/allnewsbydate.asp?NewsID=429.

[55] Harris Interactive. Most people are "privacy pragmatists" who, while concerned about privacy, will sometimes trade it off for other benefits, 2003. http://www.harrisinteractive.com/harris_poll/index.asp?PID=365.

[56] Judi Hasson. 3 principles for chief privacy officers. FCW.com, September 5, 2005. http://www.fcw.com/article90645.

[57] Geert Hofstede. *Cultures and Organizations*. McGraw-Hill, Berkshire, England, 1991.

[58] Jason I. Hong, Jennifer D. Ng, Scott Lederer, and James A. Landay. Privacy risk models for designing privacy-sensitive ubiquitous computing systems. In *Proceedings of the 2004 conference on Designing interactive systems: processes, practices, methods, and techniques*, New York, NY, August 2004. ACM Press.

[59] Michael Howard and David LeBlanc. *Writing Secure Code*. Microsoft Press, 2002.

[60] Edward Hurley. Companies creating more chief privacy officer jobs. SearchSecurity.com, January 2003. http://searchsecurity.techtarget.com/originalContent/0,289142,sid14_gci874297,00.html.

[61] IBM Corporation. Enterprise privacy authorization language (EPAL 1.2). W3C Member Submission, November 2003. http://www.w3.org/Submission/EPAL/.

[62] IBM Corporation. Platform for privacy preferences policy, downloaded March 2006. http://www.ibm.com/privacy/p3p/apps.xml.

[63] IBM Corporation. IBM WebSphere Commerce family, last visited April 2006. http://www-306.ibm.com/software/info1/websphere/index.jsp?tab=products/commerce.

[64] IBM Corporation. WebSphere Commerce 5.6.1 information center, last visited April 2006. http://publib.boulder.ibm.com/infocenter/wchelp/v5r6m1/index.jsp.

[65] IBM Corporation. Process: Shop at a hosted B2C store and Process: Order products. WebSphere Commerce 5.6.1 Information Center, last visited March 2006. http://publib.boulder.ibm.com/infocenter/wchelp/v5r6m1/topic/com.ibm.commerce.business_process.doc/concepts/processOrder_products.htm.

[66] IBM Corporation. IBM Tivoli Privacy Manager for e-business, last visited May 2006. http://www-306.ibm.com/software/tivoli/products/privacy-mgr-e-bus/.

[67] IBM Corporation. Process: Check out items (ConsumerDirect). WebSphere Commerce 5.6.1 Information Center, last visited May 2006. http://publib.boulder.ibm.com/infocenter/wchelp/v5r6m1/topic/com.ibm.commerce.business_process.doc/concepts/processCheck_out_items_(ConsumerDirect).htm.

[68] IBM Corporation. Process: Process order. WebSphere Commerce 5.6.1 Information Center, last visited May 2006. http://publib.boulder.ibm.com/infocenter/wchelp/v5r6m1/topic/com.ibm.commerce.business_process.doc/concepts/processProcess_order.htm.

[69] IBM Corporation Global Services. Privacy strategy and implementation, last visited May 2006. http://www-1.ibm.com/services/us/index.wss/offering/bcs/a1002388.

[70] Industry Canada. The challenge of change: Building the 21st century economy. Conference background paper for "e-Commerce to e-Economy: Strategies for the 21st Century", 2004. http://www.e-economy.ca/epic/internet/inec2ee-ceace.nsf/vwapj/the_challenge_of_change.pdf.

[71] International Organization for Standardization. ISO/IEC 17799:2005: Code of practice for information security management, June 2005.

[72] Carrie A. Johnson. US eCommerce overview: 2004 to 2010. Forrester Research, 2004. http://www.forrester.com/go?docid=34576.

[73] Joint Research Centre. JRC P3P resource centre. Ispra, Italy, last visited April 2006. http://p3p.jrc.it/.

[74] Jupiter Research. Seventy percent of US consumers worry about online privacy, but few take protective action, 2002. http://www.jmm.com/xp/jmm/press/2002/pr_060302.xml.

[75] Lalana Kagal, Tim Finin, Anupam Joshi, and Sol Greenspan. Security and privacy challenges in open and dynamic environments. *Computer*, 39(6):89–97, June 2006.

[76] Cem Kaner, Jack Falk, and Hung Quoc Nguyen. *Testing Computer Software*. John Wiley & Sons, Inc., New York, NY, 2nd edition, 1999.

[77] Ponnurangam Kumaraguru and Lorrie Cranor. Privacy in India: Attitutudes and awareness. In *Proceedings of the 2005 Workshop on Privacy Enhancing Technologies (PET2005)*. Dubrovnik, Croatia, June 2005.

[78] Ponnurangam Kumaraguru and Lorrie Cranor. Privacy indexes: A survey of Westin's studies. Tech. rep. CMU-ISRI-5-138, Carnegie Mellon University, December 2005.

[79] Philippa Lawson. The PIPEDA five year review: An opportunity to be grasped. *Canadian Privacy Law Review*, 3, 2005.

[80] Miriam J. Maullo and Seraphin B. Calo. Policy management: An architecture and approach. In *Proceedings of the IEEE First International Workshop on Systems Management*, Los Angeles, CA, April 1993.

[81] J.D. Meier, Alex Mackman, and Blaine Wastell. Threat modeling web applications, 2005. http://msdn.microsoft.com/library/en-us/dnpag2/html/tmwa.asp.

[82] Tamara Mendelsohn, Carrie A. Johnson, Sharyn Leaver, Nate L. Root, and Sean Meyer. The Forrester wave: Commerce platforms Q2 2005. Forrester Research, 2005. http://www.forrester.com/Research/Document/0,7211,36435,00.html.

[83] Tamara Mendelsohn, John R. Rymer, Carrie A. Johnson, and Brian Tesch. Commerce platforms: Build or buy? Forrester Research: Business Technographics, 2006. http://www.forrester.com/go?docid=38124.

[84] Microsoft Corporation. Press release: Microsoft advocates comprehensive federal privacy legislation, November 3 2005. http://www.microsoft.com/presspass/press/2005/nov05/11-03DataPrivacyPR.mspx.

[85] Sandra J. Milberg, Sandra J. Burke, H. Jeff Smith, and Ernest A. Kallman. Values, personal information privacy, and regulatory approaches. *Communications of the ACM*, 38(12):65 – 74, 1995.

[86] Object Management Group. Introduction to OMG's unified modeling language (UML), last visited June 2006. http://www.omg.org/gettingstarted/what_is_uml.htm.

[87] Office of the Privacy Commissioner of Canada. Substantially similar legislation, 2005. http://www.privcom.gc.ca/legislation/ss_index_e.asp.

[88] Dalhousie University Office of the Registrar. Undergraduate calendar 2006-2007. University Regulations, Freedom of Information and Protection of Privacy, last visited May 2006. http://www.registrar.dal.ca/calendar/ug/UREG.htm#7.

[89] Robert O'Harrow. *No Place to Hide: Behind the Scenes of Our Emerging Surveillance Society*. Simon & Schuster, Inc., 2005.

[90] Organisation for Economic Co-operation and Development. OECD guidelines on the protection of privacy and transborder flows of personal data, September 1980. http://www.oecd.org/document/18/0,2340,en_2649_34255_1815186_1_1_1_1,00.html.

[91] Organisation for Economic Co-operation and Development. Citizens as partners: Information, consultation and public participation in policy making, 2001. http://www1.oecd.org/publications/e-book/4201131E.PDF.

[92] Organisation for Economic Co-operation and Development. About OECD, last visited February 2006. http://www.oecd.org/about/0,2337,en_2649_201185_1_1_1_1_1,00.html.

[93] Organisation for Economic Co-operation and Development. OECD privacy statement generator, last visited May 2006. http://www.oecd.org/sti/privacygenerator.

[94] Ron Patton. *Software Testing*. SAMS, 2nd edition, 2005.

[95] Don Peppers and Martha Rogers. What's the deal with seals? 1to1 Media, March 2006. http://www.1to1media.com/View.aspx?DocID=29441&m=n.

[96] POLLARA. Public trust index 2000, 2000. http://www.pollara.ca/LIBRARY/Reports/trustindex.htm.

[97] Primedius Corporation. Enterprise privacy, last visited May 2006. http://www.primedius.com/Enterprise/EnterprisePrivacy.htm.

[98] Privacy Commissioner of Canada. Annual report: Privacy commissioner 1990-1991, Government of Canada, 1991. http://www.privcom.gc.ca/information/ar/02_04_01c_e.pdf.

[99] Privacy Commissioner of Canada. Annual report to Parliament: 2000-2001, Government of Canada, 2001. http://www.privcom.gc.ca/information/ar/02_04_09_e.asp.

[100] George Radwanski. Condition critical: Health privacy in Canada today. Privacy Commissioner of Canada, speech at "Meeting New Standards for Managing Privacy of Health Information", 2001. http://www.privcom.gc.ca/speech/02_05_a_010618_e.asp.

[101] Roy Morgan Research. Community attitudes to privacy. Office of the Federal Privacy Commissioner, Australia, 2001. http://www.privacy.gov.au/publications/rcommunity.html.

[102] Adam Sarner and Eugenio M. Alvarez. Business-to-consumer e-commerce magic quadrant 1Q05. Gartner Research, April 2005. http://www.gartner.com/DisplayDocument?doc_cd=126679.

[103] David Megginson SAX Project. SAX, last visited November 2005. http://www.saxproject.org/.

[104] Michael Smit, Darshanand Khusial, and Terry Chu. Increasing trust in your WebSphere Commerce site by deploying a P3P policy. IBM developerWorks, November 2005. http://www-128.ibm.com/developerworks/websphere/library/techarticles/0511_smit/0511_smit.html.

[105] Michael Smit, Mike McAllister, and Jacob Slonim. Electronic health records: Public opinion and practicalities. In *Proceedings of NAEC 2005*, Lake Garda, Italy, October 2005.

[106] Polly Sprenger. Sun on privacy: 'Get over it'. Wired News, January 26, 1999. http://www.wired.com/news/politics/0,1283,17538,00.html.

[107] State of California. *California Information Practices Act of 1977*, Civil Code Title 1.8, Chapter 1, Section 1798, passed 1977.

[108] State of New York. *Internet Security and Privacy Act*, State Technology Law, Article II, §201-208, 2002.

[109] Statistics Canada. Survey of electronic commerce and technology. CANSIM series v2656500, v2652266, v2656397, and v2656496, 2006.

[110] Blair Stewart. Privacy impact assessments. 3/4 Privacy Law & Policy Reporter 61, July 1996.

[111] Sun Microsystems. Core J2EE patterns - intercepting filter. Core J2EE Pattern Catalog, 2002. http://java.sun.com/blueprints/corej2eepatterns/Patterns/InterceptingFilter.html.

[112] Sun Microsystems. Java Platform, Enterprise Edition (Java EE), last visisted March 2006. http://java.sun.com/javaee/.

[113] Frank Swiderski and Window Snyder. *Threat Modeling*. Microsoft Press, 2004.

[114] Patrick Thibodeau. DoubleClick settlement may affect corporate IT policies. ComputerWorld, posted April 08, 2002. http://www.computerworld.com/securitytopics/security/privacy/story/0,10801,69926,00.html.

[115] Noel M. Tichy. The knowledge revolution. *Innovative Leader*, 12(12), December 2003.

[116] Ed Trapasso. Accenture study reveals wide chasm exists between U.S. businesses and consumers regarding privacy and trust related to personal data. Accenture Press Release, January 2004. http://www.accenture.com/xd/xd.asp?it=enweb&xd=_dyn/dynamicpressrelease_691.xml.

[117] Treasury Board of Canada Secretariat. Privacy impact assessment guidelines: A framework to manage privacy risks, 2002. http://www.tbs-sct.gc.ca/pubs_pol/ciopubs/pia-pefr/paipg-pefrld_e.asp.

[118] Treasury Board of Canada Secretariat. Privacy impact assessment policy, 2002. http://www.tbs-sct.gc.ca/pubs_pol/ciopubs/pia-pefr/paip-pefr_e.asp.

[119] Truste.org. TRUSTe: Make privacy your choice, last visited May 2006. http://truste.org.

[120] Voltage Security. Enterprise privacy management - Voltage data privacy solution, last visited May 2006. http://www.voltage.com/products/platform.htm.

[121] Alan F. Westin. *Privacy and Freedom.* Atheneum, 1967.

[122] whatis.com. Define policy-based management, last visited April 2006. http://whatis.techtarget.com/definition/0,,sid9_gci537241,00.html.

[123] Wikipedia. Privacy policy — wikipedia, the free encyclopedia, last visited April 2006. http://en.wikipedia.org/w/index.php?title=Privacy_policy&oldid=57101289.

[124] Wikipedia. Software testing — wikipedia, the free encyclopedia, last visited April 2006. http://en.wikipedia.org/w/index.php?title=Software_testing&oldid=47984009.

[125] Wikipedia. Hippocratic oath — wikipedia, the free encyclopedia, last visited March 2006. http://en.wikipedia.org/w/index.php?title=Hippocratic_Oath&oldid=58809871.

[126] Wikipedia. Interface (java) — wikipedia, the free encyclopedia, last visited March 2006. http://en.wikipedia.org/w/index.php?title=Interface_%28Java%29&oldid=57110352.

[127] Wikipedia. Policy — wikipedia, the free encyclopedia, last visited March 2006. http://en.wikipedia.org/w/index.php?title=Policy&oldid=41372236.

[128] Wikipedia. Solicitor-client privilege — wikipedia, the free encyclopedia, last visited May 2006. http://en.wikipedia.org/w/index.php?title=Solicitor-client_privilege&oldid=50390009.

[129] Wikipedia. Workflow — wikipedia, the free encyclopedia, last visited May 2006. http://en.wikipedia.org/w/index.php?title=Workflow&oldid=58212120.

[130] World Wide Web Consortium. The platform for privacy preferences 1.0 (P3P1.0) specification, 2002. http://www.w3.org/TR/P3P/.

[131] World Wide Web Consortium. The platform for privacy preferences 1.1 (P3P1.1) specification, 2006. http://www.w3.org/TR/P3P11/.

[132] World Wide Web Consortium. Extensible markup language (XML) 1.0 (third edition), February 2004. http://www.w3.org/TR/REC-xml/.

[133] World Wide Web Consortium. Platform for privacy preferences (P3P) project, last visited April 2006. http://www.w3.org/P3P/.

[134] World Wide Web Consortium. The extensible stylesheet language family (XSL), last visited March 2006. http://www.w3.org/Style/XSL/.

[135] World Wide Web Consortium. XSL transformations (XSLT) version 1.0. W3C Recommendation, November 1999. http://www.w3.org/TR/xslt.

[136] Raymond J. Ziegler. Business policies and decision making. In *Meredith Publishing Company*, New York, N.Y., 1966.

Appendix A

XML Schema Documents (XSD)

A.1 IFML XSD

```xml
<?xml version="1.0" encoding="ISO-8859-1" ?>
<xs:schema xmlns:xs="http://www.w3.org/2001/XMLSchema">

<xs:element name="ifml">
  <xs:complexType>
    <xs:sequence>
      <xs:element name="application_subset" maxOccurs="
          unbounded" minOccurs="0" type="application_subsetType
          "/>
    </xs:sequence>
  </xs:complexType>
</xs:element>

<xs:complexType name="application_subsetType">
  <xs:sequence maxOccurs="unbounded" minOccurs="0">
    <xs:element name="source" maxOccurs="unbounded" minOccurs
        ="0" type="entityType" />
    <xs:element name="destination" maxOccurs="unbounded"
        minOccurs="0" type="entityType" />
    <xs:element name="rule" maxOccurs="unbounded" minOccurs
        ="0" type="ruleType" />
  </xs:sequence>
  <xs:attribute name="name" type="xs:string" use="required"/>
</xs:complexType>

<xs:complexType name="entityType">
  <xs:sequence maxOccurs="unbounded" minOccurs="0">
    <xs:element name="data" maxOccurs="unbounded"
        minOccurs="0" type="dataType" />
  </xs:sequence>
  <xs:attribute name="name" type="xs:string" use="required"/>
</xs:complexType>

<xs:complexType name="dataType">
  <xs:simpleContent>
    <xs:extension base="xs:string">
      <xs:attribute name="label" type="xs:string" use="
          required"/>
      <xs:attribute name="descriptor" type="xs:string" use="
          optional"/>
      <xs:attribute name="secure" type="xs:string" default
          ="0"/>
      <xs:attribute name="sensitivity" type="xs:integer"/>
      <xs:attribute name="special" type="xs:string"/>
    </xs:extension>
  </xs:simpleContent>
</xs:complexType>
<xs:complexType name="ruleType">
```

```
    <xs:simpleContent>
      <xs:extension base="xs:string">
        <xs:attribute name="message" type="xs:string" use="
           optional"/>
        <xs:attribute name="name" type="xs:string" use="required
           "/>
        <xs:attribute name="result" type="resultType" use="
           required"/>
      </xs:extension>
    </xs:simpleContent>
  </xs:complexType>

  <xs:simpleType name="resultType">
    <xs:restriction base="xs:string">
      <xs:enumeration value="warning"/>
      <xs:enumeration value="error"/>
      <xs:enumeration value="pass"/>
      <xs:enumeration value="unknown"/>
    </xs:restriction>
  </xs:simpleType>

</xs:schema>
```

A.2 XSD Describing Mapping Files

```
<?xml version="1.0" encoding="ISO-8859-1" ?>
<xs:schema xmlns:xs="http://www.w3.org/2001/XMLSchema">

<xs:element name="mappings">
  <xs:complexType>
    <xs:sequence>
      <xs:element name="mapping" maxOccurs="unbounded"
         minOccurs="0" type="mappingType"/>
    </xs:sequence>
  </xs:complexType>
</xs:element>

<xs:complexType name="mappingType">
  <xs:sequence>
    <xs:element name="standard" type="standardType" maxOccurs
       ="1" minOccurs="1"/>
    <xs:element name="descriptor" type="xs:string" maxOccurs="
       unbounded" minOccurs="1"/>
  </xs:sequence>
</xs:complexType>

<xs:complexType name="standardType">
  <xs:simpleContent>
    <xs:extension base="xs:string">
      <xs:attribute name="sensitivity" type="xs:string" />
    </xs:extension>
  </xs:simpleContent>
</xs:complexType>

</xs:schema>
```

Appendix B
XML Stylesheet Documents (XSLs)

The following documents are XML stylesheet documents that can be used to display IFML files dynamically or to generate a set of static files from an IFML privacy compliance report.

B.1 Overview Stylesheet

```
<?xml version="1.0" encoding="ISO-8859-1"?>
<xsl:stylesheet version="1.0"
xmlns:xsl="http://www.w3.org/1999/XSL/Transform">
<xsl:template match="/">
  <html>
  <head>
    <link href="test.css" media="screen" rel="Stylesheet" type
       ="text/css" />
    <title>IFML: Summary</title>
  </head>
  <body>
  <p class='heading'>Overview</p>
    <table border="1" cellspacing="0">
  <xsl:for-each select="priml/application_subset">
    <tr bgcolor="#ffffff">
        <xsl:variable name="application_subsetName"><xsl:value-
           of select="@name"/></xsl:variable>
        <td><a href="{$application_subsetName}.html"><strong><xsl:
           value-of select="@name"/></strong></a></td>
      <xsl:for-each select="rule">
        <xsl:variable name="message"><xsl:value-of select="
           @message"/></xsl:variable>
          <xsl:choose>
            <xsl:when test="@result = 'fail'">
              <td bgcolor="#ee0000" align='center' title='{
                 $message}'><xsl:value-of select="@name"/></td>
            </xsl:when>
            <xsl:when test="@result = 'warning'">
              <td bgcolor="#eeee00" align='center'><xsl:value-of
                 select="@name"/></td>
            </xsl:when>
            <xsl:otherwise>
              <td bgcolor="#00ee00" align='center'><xsl:value-of
                 select="@name"/></td>
            </xsl:otherwise>
          </xsl:choose>
      </xsl:for-each>
    </tr>
  </xsl:for-each>
    </table>
</xsl:template>
</xsl:stylesheet>
```

B.2 Detailed Overview Stylesheet

```xml
<?xml version="1.0" encoding="ISO-8859-1"?>
<xsl:stylesheet version="1.0"
xmlns:xsl="http://www.w3.org/1999/XSL/Transform">
<xsl:template match="/">
  <html>
  <head>
    <link href="test.css" media="screen" rel="Stylesheet" type
       ="text/css" />
    <title>IFML: Detailed Summary</title>
  </head>
  <body>
  <p class='heading'>Detailed Overview</p>
  <xsl:for-each select="priml/application_subset">
   <xsl:variable name="componentName"><xsl:value-of select="
      @name"/></xsl:variable>
   <p class='title'><a href="{$componentName}.html">Component
      : <xsl:value-of select="@name"/></a></p>
   <table border="1" cellspacing="0">
   <tr bgcolor="#ffffff">
     <th align="left">Name</th>
     <th align="left">Result</th>
     <th align="left">Message</th>
   </tr>
   <xsl:for-each select="rule">
   <tr>
     <td><xsl:value-of select="@name"/></td>
       <xsl:choose>
         <xsl:when test="@result = 'fail'">
            <td bgcolor="#ee0000" align='center'><xsl:value-of
               select="@result"/></td>
         </xsl:when>
         <xsl:when test="@result = 'warning'">
          <td bgcolor="#eeee00" align='center'><xsl:value-of
             select="@result"/></td>
         </xsl:when>
         <xsl:otherwise>
            <td bgcolor="#00ee00" align='center'><xsl:value-of
               select="@result"/></td>
         </xsl:otherwise>
       </xsl:choose>
     <td><xsl:value-of select="@message"/></td>
   </tr>
   </xsl:for-each>
   </table>
  </xsl:for-each>
  <br /><br />
  <div class='footer'>
  This view was generated from IFML.<br />
  </div>
  </body>
  </html>
</xsl:template>
</xsl:stylesheet>
```

B.3 Individual Component View Stylesheet

```xml
<?xml version="1.0" encoding="ISO-8859-1"?>
<xsl:stylesheet version="1.0"
```

```xml
xmlns:xsl="http://www.w3.org/1999/XSL/Transform">
<xsl:param name='application_subset' select="ShowNothing" />
<xsl:template match="/priml/application_subset[@name=
    $application_subset]">
<html>
  <head>
      <link href="test.css" media="screen" rel="Stylesheet" type
        ="text/css" />
      <title>IFML: Detailed View: <xsl:value-of select="@name
        "/></title>
  </head>
  <body>
<p class='heading'><xsl:value-of select="@name"/></p>
<p class='title'>Information Flow</p>
<table cellpadding="0" cellspacing="0">
    <tr id="filler">
        <td> </td>
        <td> </td>
        <td class='application' rowspan="50">Application</td>
        <td> </td>
        <td> </td>
    </tr>
    <xsl:for-each select="source">
        <tr>
            <xsl:variable name='name'><xsl:value-of select="@name
                "/></xsl:variable>
            <td class='entity'><xsl:value-of select="@name"/></td>
            <td class='arrow'>
                <xsl:for-each select="data">
                    <xsl:sort select='@sensitivity' order="descending
                        " data-type="number" />
                    <xsl:sort select='@name' order="ascending" data-
                        type="text" />
                    <xsl:variable name='sensitivity'><xsl:value-of
                        select="@sensitivity"/></xsl:variable>
                    <span class='level{$sensitivity}'><xsl:value-of
                        select="@name"/>
                        <xsl:choose>
                            <!-- newest session first -->
                            <xsl:when test="@secure = '1'">
                                <img src='images/secure.gif' />
                            </xsl:when>
                        </xsl:choose>
                    <br/></span>
                </xsl:for-each>
            </td>
            <xsl:for-each select="../destination[@name = $name]">
                <td class='arrow'>
                    <xsl:for-each select="data">
                        <xsl:sort select='@sensitivity' order="
                            descending" data-type="number" />
                        <xsl:sort select='@name' order="ascending" data
                            -type="text" />
                        <xsl:variable name='sensitivity'><xsl:value-of
                            select="@sensitivity"/></xsl:variable>
                        <xsl:variable name='appName'><xsl:value-of
                            select="@appName"/></xsl:variable>
                        <span class='level{$sensitivity}'><a name='{
                            $name}' title='{$appName}'><xsl:value-of
                            select="@name"/></a>
                            <xsl:choose>
                                <!-- newest session first -->
                                <xsl:when test="@secure = '1'">
                                    <img src='images/secure.gif' />
```

```
                    </xsl:when>
                  </xsl:choose>
                  <br/></span>
                </xsl:for-each>
              </td>
              <td class='entity'><xsl:value-of select="@name"/> </
                td>
            </xsl:for-each>
          </tr>
          <tr><td colspan="5" height="10"></td></tr>
    </xsl:for-each>
      </table>
<p class='title'>Rule-based Analysis</p>
      <table border="1" cellspacing="0">
      <tr bgcolor="#ffffff">
        <th align="left">Name</th>
        <th align="left">Result</th>
        <th align="left">Message</th>
      </tr>
      <xsl:for-each select="rule">
        <tr>
          <td><xsl:value-of select="@name"/></td>
            <xsl:choose>
              <xsl:when test="@result = 'fail'">
                 <td bgcolor="#ee0000" align='center'><xsl:value-of
                    select="@result"/></td>
              </xsl:when>
              <xsl:when test="@result = 'warning'">
                <td bgcolor="#eeee00" align='center'><xsl:value-of
                    select="@result"/></td>
              </xsl:when>
              <xsl:otherwise>
                  <td bgcolor="#00ee00" align='center'><xsl:value-of
                    select="@result"/></td>
              </xsl:otherwise>
            </xsl:choose>
            <td><xsl:value-of select="@message"/></td>
        </tr>
      </xsl:for-each>
      </table>
      <br /><br />
      <div class='footer'>
      This view was generated from IFML.<br />
      </div>
      </body>
      </html>
</xsl:template>
</xsl:stylesheet>
```

VDM
Verlag Dr. Müller

Wissenschaftlicher Buchverlag bietet

kostenfreie

Publikation

von aktuellen

wissenschaftlichen Arbeiten

Diplomarbeiten, Magisterarbeiten, Master und Bachelor Theses
sowie Dissertationen und wissenschaftliche Monographien

innerhalb von Fachbuchprojekten
(Monographien und Sammelwerke)

in den Fachgebieten Wirtschafts- und Sozialwissenschaften
sowie Wirtschaftsinformatik.

Sie verfügen über eine Arbeit zu aktuellen Fragestellungen aus den genannten Fachgebieten, die hohen inhaltlichen und formalen Ansprüchen genügt, und haben **Interesse an einer honorarvergüteten Publikation**?

Dann senden Sie bitte erste Informationen über sich und Ihre Arbeit per Email an info@vdm-verlag.de. Unser Außenlektorat meldet sich umgehend bei Ihnen.

VDM Verlag Dr. Mueller e.K. · Dudweiler Landstraße 125a
D - 66123 Saarbrücken · www.vdm-buchverlag.de